D0999264

WHAT DOES GOD WANT YOU

TO DO BEFORE YOU DIE?

WHAT DOES GOD WANT YOU

TO DO BEFORE YOU DIE?

A DEVOTIONAL

Callie Daruk

CrossLink Publishing

Copyright © 2020 Callie Daruk

All rights reserved. No part of this publication may be reproduced, distributed or transmitted in any form or by any means, including photocopying, recording, or other electronic or mechanical methods, without the prior written permission of the publisher, except in the case of brief quotations embodied in critical reviews and certain other non-commercial uses permitted by copyright law. For permission requests, write to the publisher, addressed "Attention: Permissions Coordinator," at the address below.

CrossLink Publishing
1601 Mt. Rushmore Rd, STE 3288
Rapid City, SD 57702

Ordering Information:
Quantity sales. Special discounts are available on quantity purchases by corporations, associations, and others. For details, contact the "Special Sales Department" at the address above.

What Does God Want You To Do Before You Die?/Daruk —1st ed.

ISBN 978-1-63357-302-4

Library of Congress Control Number: 9781633573024

First edition: 10 9 8 7 6 5 4 3 2 1

Scripture quotations marked "CSB" are taken from the Christian Standard Bible, Copyright © 2017 by Holman Bible Publishers. Used by permission. Christian Standard Bible®, and CSB® are federally registered trademarks of Holman Bible Publishers, all rights reserved.

Scripture quotations marked "KJV" are taken from the Holy Bible, King James Version (Public Domain).

Praise for *What Does God Want You to do Before You Die?*

"We are grateful that Callie Daruk has responded to the divine whisper to pen this book, *What Does God Want You to Do Before You Die?* Her gripping personal story written skillfully in these pages, and how she was prompted to tell it, will inspire others to use their gifts to testify of God's guidance and goodness."

-**Steve & Annie Chapman**, award-winning musicians and authors of more than forty books, including A Look at Life from a Deer Stand, The Hunter's Cookbook, and the Mother-In-Law Dance.

"With her conversational writing style, Callie Daruk makes herself transparent as she invites us into her life and challenges us to inspect our own lives. Joining her on a journey of prayer and introspection, we must answer for ourselves what God wants us to do with our lives, and then, with her guidance and encouragement, we turn those dreams and goals into reality."

-**Sharon Wilharm** - Christian Filmmaker, Inspirational Speaker, and Women's Ministry Leader

"What should I do before I die? A necessary and useful question that Callie unearths and one we should ask on a regular basis. With a straightforward approach, relevant examples, and pointed takeaways, Callie gently nudges the reader towards clarity and helps to crystallize what the Lord would have each of us accomplish before we die. She then offers valuable steps on how to practically move forward into obedience of those calls. This book is a beautiful, moving tribute born out of her struggles."

-**Jess Ronne,** author of Sunlight Burning at Midnight

"Sharing the most intense moments of her life with frankness and courage, Callie offers all of us glimpses into the frailty of life and the victory of faith in the midst of it all. An inspiring, emotional, and hopeful devotional for anyone who needs a new sense of purpose for their life."

-**Gina Adams**, founder of The Adams Group Public Relations and Marketing

"Like a dear friend should, Callie gently nudges and directs us through scripture to help us discover what God has purposed us to do. If you are desperate to have your life transformed to be used for His glory - you need to read this book. It will not disappoint."

-**Dawn Owens,** award-winning author and speaker

"With humility and grace Callie Daruk prompts us all to ask, *What does God want you to do before you die?* Daruk beautifully guides readers on an examination of the heart with Biblical truth and thought-provoking calls to action. Time well spent and a lovely place to dwell! "

-**Lauren H. Brandenburg**, author of The Death of Mungo Blackwell and the middle-grade series The Books of the Gardener

"In *What Does God Want You to Do Before You Die,* author Callie Daruk issues challenge for us all. More than that, she gives what we we need to tackle that challenge. Through her own experiences and with a foundation of biblical teaching, the reader is equipped and encouraged. This is a book that will have a honored place on my shelf of favorites and one that I know I'll give as gifts again and again."

-**Edie Melson**, Director of the Blue Ridge Mountains Christian Writers Conference

"It's a subject we love to avoid, but the reality is that death comes to everyone. Perhaps we should, instead, be very intentional about living fully in God's calling. Author Callie Daruk offers both practical and spiritual guidelines for this in her new 30-day devotional "What Does God Want You to Do Before You Die?" It's an important question worth our time praying over and pondering. And this gifted storyteller prods the reader to make positive choices in difficult situations --- to be proactive in living out our unique stories. As a young person who has lived through the fragility of life, Daruk vulnerably shares her own struggles in determining how to embrace both obedience and faith in the hardest of circumstances. I suggest you savor each day slowly, and take time to work through your own answers to the application questions at the end of each devotion. The result may just be a courageous living in God's purpose and power!"

-**Lucinda Secrest McDowell**, author "Life-Giving Choices" and "Soul Strong"

"I firmly believe that everything happens for a reason and that, if we're paying attention, some of the smallest moments can create the largest ripples of impact in our lives, in the lives of others, and in our world. One such moment happened in March 2019 when my friend Ben Nemtin was the guest speaker at our cityCURRENT events in Nashville, Tennessee. Author Callie Daruk, as you'll read throughout this book, was an attendee; and she not only personally took Ben's story and words to heart, but she now has reframed the context and refocused the lens to give them a different significance and level of RESPONSIBILITY.

There is nothing more powerful than knowing and living out your PURPOSE. I'm blessed to see this through our cityCURRENT efforts each day, as we work with so many individuals and organizations to "power the GOOD" in our communities; but unfortunately, I also see so many who are lost and searching for meaning, a higher purpose, and stronger relationship with God. This book offers us a roadmap to find that higher purpose and take action to live it out; to create urgency and to make it a responsibility not just for ourselves, but for others; and most importantly, to draw closer to God and understand why we were given life on this earth. As a human and especially as a Christian, understanding our WHY is powerful and life-changing. So, that's why it's extremely humbling to have a role in something this BIG and why I challenge you to take this book and these words to heart, *What does God want you to do before you die?*"

-**Jeremy C. Park**, CEO, cityCURRENT, TV, radio and podcast producer/host, author and speaker

"Sometimes we're so busy living our lives that we forget to think about the purpose of our lives. Callie Dark's book What Does God Want You to Do Before You Die? gives a poignant reminder that God does have a plan for us, and her thoughtful stories, tips, and questions will empower us to fulfill that plan."

-**Michelle Cox**, award-winning author of the When God Calls the Heart series and Just 18 Summers

"I know with certainty that we were all created by God on purpose and with a purpose. This amazing work by Callie Daruk will reignite the fire within to pursue that purpose and to not waste a single God-given breath. You'll be encouraged to run with perseverance the race set before you like never before"

-**Stacy Edwards**, author, Devotions from the Front Porch and Devotions from the Kitchen Table, Thomas Nelson

"We at the Jerry Jenkins Writers Guild couldn't be prouder of Callie Daruk for penning this challenging, convicting, and ultimately enriching book. You'll find it inspiring!"

–**Jerry B. Jenkins**, Novelist & biographer

"What does God want me to do before I die? This question, which we all ask, author Callie Daruk graciously and wisely answers in her first lyrical, heartfelt devotional. From her days knocking on doors as a soul-winning girl in Kentucky to watching her infant son fighting for his life, Callie uses her personal journey to lead her readers into deeper spiritual truths. This devotional was timely as our family transitions out of a season of healing. I am grateful I found it when I did."

-**Jolina Petersheim**, bestselling author of How the Light Gets In

"Thirty days and one easy question. Or is it? Perhaps it gets deeper to the heart of man than most. At least it got to the heart of this reader. Callie Daruk's timely book reminds me that this span of my lifetime is not about what I want to do (although that list is long), but about what God wants me to do. This book is a keeper ... and one I can't wait to purchase for my friends. "

-**Eva Marie Everson**, Bestselling Author & Speaker, President, Word Weavers International

To my precious husband, Frank, who has loved me as Christ has loved the church since the day our eyes first met – unconditional and sacrificial. I love you more with each passing day.

To my mighty arrows, Elijah, Isaiah, and Joshua – through you, the most incredible role of my life unfolded and the sweetest name I'll ever hear was uttered – Mom.

Daruk men, loving you is the greatest thing I'll ever do before I die.

Contents

INTRODUCTION

What shall I do, Lord?
—Acts 22:10 KJV

All heaven lies before the grasp of the asking man...
—Charles Spurgeon

The question glared at me from the screen as I awaited the morning's keynote speaker. I'd never heard of Ben Nemtin but judging by the roar of the audience as he approached the platform, I was the only one.

With great passion and poise, Ben shared the epic story of how, following a serious battle with depression and through a series of unlikely events, he and three friends got together to create a television show, *The Buried Life*. Inspired by a line in an old poem, the show consisted of four guys with an old video camera and an even older van who embarked on a quest to answer one simple question:

What do you want to do before you die?

Together the friends made a checklist of random and seemingly impossible things they'd like to accomplish before they died. What began as a journey of four college-age guys getting to do some really cool stuff soon became much bigger than themselves.

Moved by people they met along the way with dreams and needs as big as their own, they made a decision that changed everything. For every item they crossed off their own bucket lists, they were going to find someone else and help them cross something off theirs.

I joined in the crowd's laughter and shared in their tears as Ben told tale after tale of touching heart after heart. Armed with little more than sheer will, determination, and persistence, they watched the impossible become possible one story at a time.

As Ben continued, my heartbeat sped. Again, he asked:

"What do you want to do before you die?"

I heard his thought-provoking question but, in my heart, I immediately heard a more personal one.

Callie, what do I want you to do before you die?

Though an inaudible whisper, I recognized God's voice and I heard his question loud and clear. Just that morning in quiet time he'd posed a similar one.

Callie, what did I call you to do?
You called me to write the book, Lord.
So, lets write it.

Three years earlier I'd started writing my memoir but, as it has a way of doing, self-doubt creeped in and I set my manuscript aside. Reliving the trauma of the past coupled with the uncertainty that anyone would want to read what I had to say inevitably caused my flow of words to wane. As the Lord gently spoke to my heart that morning, I had no idea that he was preparing me for the speech I was about to hear.

Before a standing ovation and a barrage of cheers, Ben asked his question one last time.

"What do you want to do before you die?"

And, one last time, my heart heard:

What does God want you to do before you die?

Plastered on a wall in the back of the room were dozens of fill-in-the-blank sentences that audience members were given the opportunity to complete.

"Before I die, I want to _____."

Without hesitation I grabbed the dry erase marker and wrote, "Write the book." God and I both knew what book. And, though the marks were erasable, somehow seeing it on that board made my commitment permanent. From the corner of my eye I saw Ben standing in front of the wall smiling and posing with people. I made my way towards him and the photographer snapped a photo of us. I shook Ben's hand and thanked him knowing the image he'd left on my heart would outlive any photo.

The question followed me, and for days I could think of little else. Each morning as I'd read my Bible, verses related to time glowed from the page. In news headlines, on the television, and in conversations, signs of the times surrounded me as I fought for a reason not to ask myself this important question and make my own list.

The same signs are surrounding you and I imagine you feel them too. I hear your heart's cry to accomplish the dreams and the callings God has purposed for your life—but I also hear its excuses:

It's too late.
I'm too old.
I've messed up too badly.
I've done _____ so God can't use me.

I hear them so clearly because they're joining the choir of my own.

When my children were young there were plenty of foul odors to go around, but one of the worst smells I noticed was when they'd leave a sippy cup full of milk in the car. I never understood how they wedged those cups into so many hidden places, but they always managed it. At first, the odor would be strong and I'd recognize it right away. I'd smell it every time I got in the car, but over time I got used to it. Eventually, I'd find the old cup with the putrid milk and throw it out.

Today—right here, right now—let's write down all the excuses and all the lies the enemy has spoon fed us over a lifetime. At the end of this introduction, you'll notice a blank page. Take a moment and think about the lies that always get you. As you read through this book, if any come to your mind, go back to the blank page and write them down. Go back to them periodically, read them, and let their stench be like that sour old sippy cup. My earnest prayer is that by the end of this book, together, we will be ready to throw those stinky excuses away for good.

It's time to take a long, hard look at ourselves. As Christians, have we asked what it is we're supposed to be doing? Have we accomplished what we set out to accomplish? What are the gifts and callings God has placed on our lives, and are we using them? The sands of time are dropping, Beloved, and no matter how hard we try, we cannot stop or even slow their descent.

Ben's single question is inspiring millions around the globe, and rightfully so. It is a very important question to ask, but as Christians I cannot help but think of one far greater that we need to be asking ourselves:

 What does God want you to do before you die?

Notes

_____

_____

_____

_____

_____

_____

_____

_____

_____

_____

_____

_____

CALLED TO ACTION

Even so faith, if it hath not works, is dead,
being alone.
—James 2:17 KJV

Saying and doing are two different things.
—Matthew Henry

"Dreams have a way of staying dreams." A quick glimpse into my past proved the words from Ben Nemtin's speech to be true. I'd made my own list once, but it wasn't at all like the one from *The Buried Life*. Instead, mine was a list of all the things I'd started and stopped over the years—things I'd dreamed of doing but failed miserably at. It wasn't pretty and it wasn't short either.

What was it that made Ben and his friends so successful at reaching their seemingly unattainable goals? How were they able to play basketball at the White House with the President of the United States? How did they anchor the evening news, talk to Oprah Winfrey, and write a New York Times bestseller? One by one they made the impossible possible, but how?

The list was the first critical step. When it comes to making lists, I could easily be the world's worst. No expense is spared as I find the cutest notepad and the nicest pen to craft my lofty list. Inevitably, when I arrive at my destination, I realize I left it at home. By itself, my list did little good.

For Ben and his friends, writing down what they wanted to accomplish was essential—but the most important step they made was to *do something.* Unlike many of my planned endeavors, they took action.

I knew the question that had been burning in my heart since hearing Ben's speech, but I hadn't actually asked it.

What do you want me to do before I die, Lord?

Thoughts and ideas came to my mind as I asked him, and I began writing them down. Rome wasn't built in a day, so I started with what I knew: finishing the book. But that would mean I'd have to take it seriously; I'd need to start making some goals and setting some deadlines.

Rome also wasn't built alone, so I decided to reach out to others. While browsing my Facebook profile one day, I noticed my friend count.

Maybe they can help me.

Determined to finish what I knew God had called me to do, I made a bold step: I posted my manuscript word count along with a commitment of writing five hundred words per day and three thousand words per week. Each week I posted my word count and asked for prayer as I worked towards my goal.

I didn't want this dream to stay a dream. More importantly, I knew God didn't either.

"Callie, do you want to write a book?"

If someone were to have asked me that, my answer would've been a resounding yes. However, with pleasing myself and the satisfaction of accomplishing a goal as my sole motivation, I'm not sure it would've ever gotten done. There's little doubt it would've just been added to my growing log of unfinished tasks.

"Callie, does God want you to write a book?"

That sole question led to the completion of my thirty-thousand-word memoir in only a matter of weeks. What changed?

For one, my motivation. My *dream* shifted to my *calling*, and it was no longer optional.

Secondly, fueled by the knowledge that as Christians we are called to action, how could I not write? If actions don't follow our faith, it is useless. If actions do not follow our callings, what good will come of them? I know you have dreams and I know how badly you want to see them realized. I know you have gifts and talents and I want to see you using them. More importantly, so does God.

After taking a long, hard look inside ourselves, let's take a long, hard look around us. Life is not getting any easier and hearts are not getting any softer. How many hearts could be waiting to be softened by your calling?

Eventually, life's hourglass will empty, but this one we can't flip over with the flick of the wrist and restart. If we fail to act, the impact of our lives will be even smaller than that of our vain words.

Beginning today, at the end of each devotion you'll notice a section entitled "Called to Action." Here you'll find some tough questions, some provoking thoughts, and most importantly, a call to action. As we journey together through this book, this section will be critical. This is where the rubber meets the road, where the pen meets the paper, and hopefully where our feet hit the pavement. Each day is designed to build on the others so that by the time you finish this book you will have met two important goals:

1. Know one thing (perhaps more, but at least one) that God wants you to do before you die.
2. Be actively working towards accomplishing it.

It's going to take honesty and courage. It may require you to step out of your comfort zone, but as you do, dear friend, know that you will not go it alone.

Called to Action

Ask:

What does God want me to do before I die?

DOES MY LIFE REALLY MATTER?

For by him were all things created, that
are in heaven, and that are in earth, visible
and invisible, whether they be thrones, or
dominions, or principalities, or powers: all
things were created by him, and for him.
—Colossians 1:16 KJV

A holy life is no work of chance; it is a
masterpiece of order.
—Charles Spurgeon

Blurred streaks of evergreen trees whizzed outside the car window as fast as thoughts did inside my young mind. My brother sat to my left, my daddy drove, and momma rode beside him: a random day that my memory brings to mind, when love filled the car and questions filled my heart. Before I could even pronounce the word *philosophical*, those questions invaded my thoughts.

Why am I here?
What are we all doing here?
What is the meaning of life?

Age and uncertainty never kept me from pondering the deeper things of life. As if in response, beyond the window, stars shimmered and pointed the way to their creator—the God I always believed existed and held answers to questions I didn't quite know how to ask.

Belonging.

A glimpse into the earliest memories of my life reminded me I always craved a sense of belonging.

Acceptance.

In an epic experiment filled with failures I'd like to forget, the search for acceptance during my adolescence proved unsuccessful.

Purpose.

Like a buried treasure I'd stumble upon one day, purpose eluded me throughout most of my adult life. In job after job, I sought for meaning. Desperately—at times too desperately—I wanted to matter. I know you do too.

Without understanding and believing in our significance, we will never be able resolve the question we picked up this book to answer. If we don't believe we have a purpose—if we don't believe we matter—our question won't either.

One of my go-to chapters for remembering my worth is Psalm 139. When my insecurities scream loudly, these verses drown them out.

When I feel no one really knows me, David says of God: "Lord, you have searched me and known me."

God knows me.

When I feel no one really understands me, David says of God: "You understand my thoughts from far away."

God understands me.

When I feel alone, David says of God: "Where can I go to escape your spirit? Where can I flee from your presence? If I go up to heaven, you are there; if I make my bed in Sheol , you are there. If I live at the eastern horizon or settle at the western limits, even there your hand will lead me; your right hand will hold on to me."

God is with me.

When my life feels arbitrary and random, David says of God, "For it was you who created my inward parts; you knit me together in my mother's womb."

God made me.

When I feel myself to be worthless, David says of God, "I will praise you because I have been remarkably and wondrously made. Your works are wondrous, and I know this very well."

God made me special.

When I feel hidden, David says of God: My bones were not hidden from you when I was made in secret, when I was formed in the depths of the earth. Your eyes saw me when I was formless..."

God sees me.

When I feel my life has no purpose, David says of God: "...all my days were written in your book and planned before a single one of them began."

God has a plan for me.

When I feel no one remembers me, David says of God: "God, how precious your thoughts are to me; how vast their sum is! If I counted them, they would outnumber the grains of sand."

God thinks about me and his thoughts toward me are precious.

And finally, when I feel abandoned, David says of God: "When I wake up, I am still with you."

God never leaves me.

Your life matters and it is neither random nor arbitrary. You were planned. You were created and you have a purpose. Let's get to discovering it.

Called to Action

Ask:

Read Psalm 139 and remind yourself of these nine truths:

1. God knows me.
2. God understands me.
3. God is with me.
4. God made me.
5. God made me special.
6. God sees me.
7. God has a plan for me.
8. God thinks about me and his thoughts toward me are precious.
9. God never leaves me.

Do I believe what Psalm 139 says about me?

Do I believe God created me with great purpose?

Continue Asking:

What does God want me to do before I die?

AS GRASS

As for man, his days are as grass...
—Psalm 103:15 KJV

How short is man's life, and uncertain!
—Matthew Henry

Freshly cut grass and its distinct aroma are universal signs that the coldness of winter has bowed once again to spring's annual arrival. In due time, the grass that announced one season's arrival divulges another's exit as brown, thirsty blades speak of a summer ready to welcome the weight of falling leaves.

Two interesting things are compared to grass in the Bible:

1. Man's days: "As for man, his days are like grass - he blooms like a flower of the field; when the wind passes over it, it vanishes, and its place is no longer known" (Ps. 103:15-16 Christian Standard Bible).
2. All flesh: "All flesh is like grass, and all its glory like a flower of the grass. The grass withers, and the flower falls..." (1 Pet. 1:24; Isa. 40:6-7 CSB).

Several things come to mind as I think about the qualities of grass. For one, its changeability. Have you ever driven by someone's lush, green, and painstakingly manicured lawn? What about a rolling field sitting peacefully in the countryside with nothing more than cattle to decorate it? Grass—that's all it is, and yet its simple beauty evokes such deep emotion.

On the other hand, have you driven by someone's unmanicured lawn? Uncared for and left to draw its one and only drink from the early morning dew, it sits parched and ugly. In the heat of the day, the sound of the crunch beneath your feet reminds you that little could grow there. Devoid of proper nutrients, its weak spot exposed by summer's brutal heat, it adapts to its environment, changing its appearance even though it had potential for beauty.

Another characteristic of grass that comes to mind is its transitory nature. Land lovers across the globe get irate when corporations seek to turn beautiful landscapes into condominiums and hotels. They fight to preserve earth's beauty, but all too often their fight is in vain. Before they know it, dense pasture is exchanged for plywood and sheetrock. Here one day and gone the next.

Like grass, we change. We are temporary and, hard though we may fight for our illusion of it, we have no control over when our lives will wither like the grass blade.

What's the point, you might ask, if we are to wither like grass our days are to be blown away with the wind? Well, first let's look at grass. A quick study of its importance left me surprised. Grass has a ripple effect upon humanity and serves a tremendous purpose. Beauty aside, it covers, it sustains, and it nourishes. An ordinary, everyday thing yet it is so important.

Did you know that grass goes dormant in the winter? Dormant grass is often mistaken for dead grass. Indeed, dingy and seemingly dry, they look very much the same. But unlike dead grass, dormant grass can be revived. It can and will make a comeback and, in its proper time, become lush, green, and beautiful once more.

Though we may often feel as ordinary as grass, we each serve a tremendous purpose. As grass will see its end, so will we, Dear One. Perhaps we've felt (and even appeared to others) dried up and unrecoverable, but we've just been dormant. We cannot know when we will vanish like the grass and wither from the earth, but we can decide what we will look like while we are still here. Will we water ourselves with God's Word and be lush and useful? Or will we do nothing, believing the lie that we're dead and useless, when we're really just in a state of dormancy? If you've picked up this book, you are clearly not dead, friend. So chin up. There's still time.

Called to Action

Ask:

Is the grass of my life lush and green or dry and dingy?

Am I dormant? If yes, what is one step I can take right now to water the dry places of my heart?

These questions are so much bigger than you and me, but they must still be asked. After questioning your own heart, ask God the very same questions. That step is vital and helps us get to the heart of the issue. The Holy Spirit will guide us into truth, without which we will remain in our state of dormancy.

Continue Asking:

What does God want me to do before I die?

Begin personalizing this question. *God, what do you want me to do before I die?*

DEAD MAN WALKING

And as it is appointed unto men once to die,
but after this the judgment...
—Hebrews 9:27 KJV

We are all under a fatal necessity of dying.
—Matthew Henry

J esus was a dead man walking. Matthew 16:21, among other places, reflects his awareness of that.

"From then on, Jesus began to point out to his disciples that it was necessary for him to go to Jerusalem and suffer many things from the elders, chief priests, and scribes, *be killed,* and be raised the third day."

While Christ's death would be brief, the whole of Christianity hinged upon his mortality. Once, when Jesus tried to tell the disciples he must die, Peter did what most of us do.

"Oh no, Lord! This will never happen to you!" (Matt. 16:22 CSB).

We basically say the same thing today when others tell us they are sick or dying.

"You're going to be okay. Everything's going to be alright," we say, but how do we know that? Jesus spoke sharply in response to Peter's comment. He turned and told Peter, "Get behind me, Satan! You are a hindrance to me because you're not thinking about God's concerns but human concerns" (Matt. 16:23 CSB).

It feels rather natural to dismiss the possibility of death (or even any talk of it) but for Jesus, keeping death at the forefront of his mind was essential. His physical presence on earth was short and his time of ministry was even shorter. There was much to accomplish in three years. "What do you want me to do before I die, God," was the question and essence of Christ's entire purpose.

Jesus said, "For I have come down from heaven, not to do my own will, but the will of him who sent me" (John 6:38 CSB). At another time, after his disciples told him to eat, he responded, "My food is to do the will of him who sent me and to finish his work" (John 4:34 CSB). In the garden of Gethsemane, moments before being apprehended, beaten, and crucified, Jesus prayed, "Father, if you are willing, take this cup away from me—nevertheless, not my will, but yours, be done" (Luke 22:42 CSB).

Jesus was a dead man walking, and so are we.

In his commentary on Ecclesiastes 8, Matthew Henry says, "Death is an enemy that we must all enter the lists with sooner or later: there is no discharge in that war, no dismission from it. Death is a battle that must be fought."

Henry plainly summarizes the eighth verse of the same chapter:

> A man has no power to adjourn the day of his death, nor can he by prayers or bribes obtain a reprieve; no bail will be taken. We have not power over the spirit of a friend, to retain that; the prince, with all his authority, cannot prolong the life of the most valuable of his subjects, nor the physician with his medicines and methods, nor the soldier with his force, not the orator with his eloquence, nor the best saint with his intercessions. The stroke of death can by no means be put

by when our days are determined and the hour
appointed us has come.

As you and I set out to ask the epic question of what God
wants us to do before we die, let's pause for a moment. Can we
honestly ask that question without first realizing that we are all
dead men walking? The realization itself is the very reason for
the question. Our mortality is not something we want to give
much thought to, and death is not a popular or easy topic to dis-
cuss, but if we really want to find the answer to our question, we
must do both.

If we fail to see our appointed time of death looming and if
we assume tomorrow will always come, we may risk a fatal er-
ror: losing sight of our entire purpose. Jesus knew he was going
to die, and his awareness of death didn't hinder his purpose—it
fueled it. May it do the same in us, Beloved.

Called to Action

Ask:

Do I avoid thinking about or discussing the topic of death? Why?

Have I given recent thought to my own mortality?

*Can I say, like Jesus, that my purpose on earth is to do the will of
the Father and to finish his work?*

If that has not been your heart's cry but you want it to be, let
the acknowledgement of that be your prayer. *Oh, God. I have not
given thought to my own mortality. I have not concerned myself with
your will or your work, but I want to.*

Prayers don't always have to be long or complicated; they must
only come from the heart. Many of my own personal prayers begin with the simple acknowledgement that I am not doing as I

ought. The success of a prayer does not lie in its length; it lies in the sincere faith that utters it.

Continue Asking:

God, what do you want me to do before I die?

Don't forget about the space in the beginning of the book. Have you thought of any more lies you've believed that are hindering you from pursuing the God-given dreams and callings in your life? Take a minute and write them down.

CERTAINLY, BUT MAYBE SUDDENLY

For this God is our God for ever and ever: he will be our guide even unto death.
—Psalm 48:14 KJV

Death will come certainly, but maybe suddenly.
—Matthew Henry

One beautiful day on a crowded street in Dallas, President John F. Kennedy met with death unexpectedly. One bustling morning in Manhattan, thousands of people perished after two planes crashed into the World Trade Center. Every day, in the quiet of their bathrooms, expectant mothers miscarry. Unexpected and sudden, the losses were and continue to be great.

Both human and biblical history are replete with examples of unforeseen deaths. Scripture tells us that Lot's wife suddenly became a pillar of salt when she looked back toward Sodom and Gomorrah. Following a confrontation with Peter, Ananias and Sapphira dropped dead.

Death will come certainly and quite possibly it will come suddenly. It's a fact we all know, but it's difficult to think about, nonetheless.

"I carried a black dress with me to work because I knew I would be attending your son's funeral."

When my son, Isaiah, returned home from the hospital after three hundred and twenty-four consecutive days, one of his primary nurses who'd traveled from Lexington to Nashville to work weekends said that to my husband and me. She'd seen a lot in her years as an NICU nurse and she was certain a sudden death would be Isaiah's fate. For way too many parents in the NICU, that was the case. Over the course of a year, we met many of them and saw the devastation it brought.

Last year at my church, the youth pastor and his wife experienced the sudden loss of their beautiful two-year-old son. Happy and full of life one day, he was gone the next. The same was true for my cousin, whose sixteen-year-old son died instantly in a tragic car wreck. It is painstakingly hard to wrap our minds around these types of deaths, and yet they are all around us.

No matter how unpleasant, the possibility of sudden death is one we all face. Perhaps an unexpected death has come to someone you know or hold dear. Many times, and for many people, it results in such anger or bitterness that they shut down; they stop their work for God altogether.

Instead of dismissing the inevitable, let's begin to think about death and its uncertain timing, but do so in light of truth.

In his sermon entitled, The Wailing of Risca, Charles Spurgeon once said, "Let us learn to hold loosely our dearest friends. Let us love them, but let us always learn to love them as dying things."

Living with that awareness, though the load of it may be heavy, is the very catalyst that can turn our apathy into action. Armed with this truth, we can boldly step up. What time we have remaining is out of our control, but what we do with it is up to each of us.

Instead of being a source of great pain, we can allow this certainty to fuel us and drive us to make a decision that today—right now—we will begin to offer our lives as a living sacrifice. If God should sustain us another day, let death be a perpetual reminder that there are no guarantees; that there will not always be another day to accomplish the great work he is calling us to.

"Yes, we admit that we shall die, but not so soon as to make it a pressing matter, we imagine that we are not within measurable distance of the tomb," said Charles Spurgeon in his sermon, What is Your Life?

It is a dangerous thing to presume we will have more time. We very well may but we very well may not. Those we hold so dear very well may and they very well may not. As we talk about this, imagine with me that *suddenly* comes before *certainly*. As I do this, I wonder a few things:

1. Is my heart right before God? Am I truly his and is he truly mine? Have I surrendered the broken mess of my heart and life for the beautiful display of the truest love I'll ever know? It will be even harder to talk about death if this is not the case. Only a supernatural love could free my soul from sin and only that kind of love can help my heart understand this matter.
2. Can I say, like Paul, that I have fought the good fight? Can I say, like he could, that I've run my race and finished my course?

Don't fret, Dear One, if your answer is "No," like mine. That's exactly why I wrote this book; I imagined I would not be the only one. Let's discover, together, why the God of the marvelous and magnificent universe made a one-of-a-kind, no-one-else-the-same-on-earth, you.

Called to Action

Ask:

Has the sudden death of someone I love caused me to become angry and bitter? If someone I love were to die today, have I said everything I need to say to them?

If I were to die today, would I die pursuing God?

Continue Asking:

What do you want me to do before I die, God?

No part of these questions is easy—nor should they be—but that shouldn't keep us from asking them. Let them stir your heart in ways that may be uncomfortable. Resist the urge to move on to the next day until you're ready. Although this book covers thirty days, it may take you longer to complete it and that's perfectly okay. God is right there with you every step of the way.

FRAGILE: HANDLE WITH CARE

*For he knoweth not that which shall be; for
who can tell him when it shall be?*
—Ecclesiastes 8:7 KJV

*Nothing but a continuous miracle keeps any
one of us from the sepulcher.*
—Charles Spurgeon

Deafening alarms rang through the fourth floor, announcing that a baby had stopped breathing. Medical personnel within earshot of my son's code blue call instantly flooded his room.

"Step aside. Now!" a frantic nurse said as she darted toward us.

My husband and I were rushed to the corner of the room as they tried to resuscitate our son. I held my breath. No matter how hard they tried to resuscitate him, nothing worked. Clad in a jacket with embroidered angel wings above the phrase "Vanderbilt Life Flight Team," a petite woman rushed toward him. She straddled his isolette, interlaced her fingers, and let the whole weight of her body fall as she began chest compressions.

I held my breath, praying that somehow it could reach him. The terrifying scene unfolded before my husband and me for more than twenty minutes. Amidst the bustle of the scrub-filled room, his twin lay sleeping in his own isolette, unaware that his brother was fighting for his life.

Isaiah's monitor kept silent. Nothing was visible but straight lines that wouldn't budge. In disbelief, I stared at my son's lifeless body. As if an invisible hand pulled a sheet over him, a blue wave of death washed over his small form. It started at the top of his head and slowly covered his toes. Tears slid down nurses' faces as they worked desperately to revive him.

The oversized door that stood between the rest of the unit and our room slammed against the wall as Isaiah's doctor burst into the room.

"What did you give him?" he yelled to the nurse.

"A PRN dose of fentanyl, sir."

"Go get the Narcan, now!" he shouted.

The nurse ran out of the room in a full sprint. She returned with a syringe full of liquid and immediately the doctor pushed the medicine into Isaiah's IV port. Within seconds, we heard it.

Beep......
Beep...
Beep.

Divine waves of life appeared on the monitor. The blue sheet of death that covered my son's lifeless body was pulled back, starting at his toes this time. Radiant color washed over every inch and landed at his head. Life had returned.

I can't say I ever thought I'd experience this type of closeness with death but together, in a moment seared upon our hearts, my husband and I did. Like a scene straight out of a movie, we watched as the fragility of life unfolded before our eyes.

Often, in our brief ponderings of death, emotions arise that overwhelm us. Thoughts of our own mortality remind us of lives we've loved and lost. Too painful to relive, we shove them into the dark recesses of our hearts. Where children and sickness are involved, they seem especially unbearable. I know this all too well.

Not long after the scene I described, I found myself pacing the hallways of the critical care unit of the NICU. I felt sad and confused, yet guilty for feeling bad at the same time.

It could be so much worse.

I kept telling myself that, but it didn't ease the pain. A lady whom I believe to have been an angel unawares came out of nowhere and laid her hand on my shoulder. "You are where you are and it's okay to hurt," she told me.

I'd never seen or spoken to her before, but the words she spoke to me were like the hug I so desperately needed.

Perhaps you are like I was and you're hurting too badly to ask yourself some tough questions right now. That's okay too, friend. Life is fragile and so are our emotions. You are where you are and in this very moment, it's okay to hurt a while.

Called to Action

Ask:

Instead of asking yourself a question today, reflect upon where you are in your life right now. Be honest with yourself and with God about how you feel. He already knows and he deeply cares. Perhaps he's waiting patiently until you're ready to come and talk to him.

A loving father knows to give his son space to breathe, to reflect and ponder his actions. And, no matter where the son has been, when he's ready to talk the loving father embraces him, knowing all along that he'd return when he was ready.

Return to your loving heavenly Father today. Truly, this is the first step if we ever hope to answer our question and pursue our purpose.

NO GUARANTEES

...but time and chance happen to them all.
—Ecclesiastes 9:11 KJV

This is a poor withering life at the best, for we all fade as a leaf. Unless we purposely live with a view to the next world, we cannot make much out of our present existence.
—Charles Spurgeon

"If it is what I think it is, your son has twelve to twenty-four hours to live. He needs to be operated on now."

The neonatologist's announcement to my husband and me regarding our seven-week-old preemie was my first real brush with the uncertainty of life. The doctor was right, and after an intense battle to convince the surgeon to operate, my deathly-ill son was rushed to emergency surgery.

More than six hours later, another terrifying declaration came from the doctor.

"Every hour your son survives is a good hour."

I didn't want hours. I wanted days. I wanted months and years. What I wanted most were guarantees, but they couldn't offer any. Five months later, still more death-tinged words were spoken over my son by another doctor.

"Your son's liver is failing and there's nothing more we can do. Babies don't recover from this."

While most babies slept and fed, mine lay medicated and fought. He fought to live. With each brushstroke the doctors painted, a picture I didn't want to see began taking shape. Neither life nor time came with guarantees. I'd never been more aware of that fact than when my son's life hung in the balance.

In his sermon "The Death of the Christian," Charles H. Spurgeon said, "How hackneyed [cliché] is the thought that all men must die, and therefore, what can we say upon it? And yet we blush not to repeat it, for while it is a truth so well known, there is none so much forgotten; while we all believe it in the theory and receive it in the brain, how seldom it is impressed on the heart? The sight of death makes us remember it. The tolling of the solemn bell speaks to us of it. We hear the deep-tongued voice of time as the bell tolls the hours and preaches our mortality. But very usually we forget it. Death is inevitable to all."

The line that separates life and death is grass-blade thin. This hard truth permeates scripture, such as Ecclesiastes 3:1-2, which says there is "...a time to be born, and a time to die..."

A time to be born, and a time to die.

I settle on that phrase because before my son's illness, I assumed the gap that separated those two would be decades apart. I never realized how alarmingly close one could be to the other.

Solomon continues, "For he [man] knoweth not that which shall be; for who can tell him when it shall be?" (Eccl. 8:7 KJV).

Not only do we not know what will be, but no one else can tell us. How often have we all said to one another, "See you tomorrow"? What we are really saying is, in essence, "I hope I see you tomorrow." The former is a promise we may not be able to keep.

James, a servant of Christ, spoke of this truth. "Come now, you who say, 'Today or tomorrow we will travel to such and such a city and spend a year there and do business and make a profit.' Yet you do not know what tomorrow will bring—what your life will be! For you are like vapor that appears for a little while, then vanishes. Instead, you should say, 'If the Lord wills, we will live and do this or that'" (James 4:13-15 CSB).

We do not know the day or hour our time on earth will end; it simply isn't guaranteed. In a split second, our plans could change and our date with death arrive. In the twinkling of an eye, the Lord himself could descend and in that moment, the dead in Christ will rise first and those who are alive and remain will be caught up together with them in the clouds. If it occurs in our lifetime, we will meet the Lord in the air and be ever with him. In that day, death will lose its sting and the grave its victory. Fellow Christian, don't lose heart. Although the length of our time on earth comes with no guarantees, life eternal does.

Called to Action

Ask:

Do you live with the truth that tomorrow is not guaranteed impressed upon your heart?

In light of that truth, are you pursuing your purpose?

Continue Asking:

God, what do you want me to do before I die?

Is something beginning to take shape? Is there someone you need to forgive? Someone you need to help? Maybe you haven't picked up your Bible in years. Though they may seem small, they could be the very things God is waiting for you to do before you die.

PREPARED FOR DEATH

*The Son of Man must be delivered into the
hands of sinful men, and be crucified, and
the third day rise again.*
—Luke 24:7 KJV

To be prepared to die is to be prepared to live.
—Charles Spurgeon

U nderstanding death to be inevitable is one thing, but preparing for it is another. Jesus knew his purpose on earth would require death. It was a hard fact for his disciples to grasp but one they had to know. And, when the time was right, that which he'd previously only hinted at, Jesus began to reveal in full:

> *From that time forth began Jesus to show unto his disciples, how that he must go unto Jerusalem, and suffer many things of the elders and chief priests and scribes, and be killed, and be raised again the third day.* (Matthew 16:21 KJV)

Jesus's full disclosure to his disciples followed two important questions he'd just asked them:

1. "Who do people say that the Son of Man is?" (Matt. 16:13 CSB)
2. "But you," he asked them, "who do you say that I am?" (Matt. 16:15 CSB)

Peter responded to Jesus's question with full assurance that he was who he claimed to be. In his commentary of this conversation, Matthew Henry states: "All truths are not to be spoken to all persons at all times, but such as are proper and suitable to their present state." Perhaps the disciples hadn't been ready to hear what needed to be said any earlier. Maybe their hearts wouldn't have grasped it just yet.

"Your twins are right on the cusp at only thirty weeks. Things could go really well, or they could go really bad. Time will tell."

The neonatologist tried her best to prepare my husband and me for what lay ahead. I wasn't ready to hear what the doctor told me but regardless, it was time to hear it. In the garden of Gethsemane that night, Jesus's time arrived. The moment he'd tried to prepare his disciples' hearts for was at hand.

He'd taught them, instructed them, corrected and warned them, all in preparation for the fact that not only would he suffer, but for his name's sake, they would suffer too. They were the ones to carry on Christ's work and they needed to be ready.

In reading this story, I noticed that Jesus didn't just prepare the hearts of those around him for his death, he also prepared his own. Three times in the garden of Gethsemane when his time was near at hand, he fell on his face and prayed. Peter and the other men with him were supposed to be watching. Instead, they slept.

"O my Father, if it be possible, let this cup pass from me: nevertheless, not as I will, but as thou wilt." (Matt. 26:39 KJV)

With exceeding sorrow, Jesus cried out to his Father. He prepared for his death by submitting to his Father's will. Again, he prayed, "O my Father, if this cup may not pass away from me, except I drink it, thy will be done." With an awareness of what was to come and with prayer so intense he sweat drops of blood, his heart was preparing to accomplish his mission. A third time he prayed the same words, and at last his time had come. In vain would we attempt to find a more important example of preparing for death.

Maybe in the past you've not given much thought to preparing for death. As Mr. Henry stated, maybe, like the disciples, you hadn't been in the "proper and suitable state" to consider it, but now you are. You are growing, maturing, and you hear the call to prepare.

If Jesus hadn't been prepared to suffer and die, he may not have. Had Jesus not prepared the disciples to go into all of the world, they may not have. If you and I don't prepare our hearts for God's call on our lives, what might go undone?

As we prepare, Precious Saint, we don't prepare alone. In fact, Jesus is still preparing. Once again, he's preparing something for you.

> Don't let your heart be troubled. Believe in God; believe also in me. In my Father's house are many rooms; if not, I would have told you. I am going away to prepare a place for you. If I go away and prepare a place for you, I will come again and take you to myself, so that where I am you may be also." (John 14:1-3 CSB)

Called to Action

Ask:

Have I been like Peter and the other men, sleeping instead of watching?

Am I at a place in my life to understand the importance of death and the significance of preparing for it?

Continue Asking:

What do you want me to do before I die, God?

IT'S OKAY TO TALK ABOUT DEATH

A good name is better than precious ointment; and the day of death than the day of one's birth.
—Ecclesiastes 7:1 KJV

"...our going out of the world is as great a kindness to us than our coming into the world was."
—Matthew Henry

6 99.
That's the number of times the King James version of the Bible mentions the words *death*, *die*, and *dying*. In one particular occurrence, I was stunned as I read: "A good name is better than precious ointment; and the day of death than the day of one's birth" (Eccles. 7:1).

Our day of death is better than our day of birth? That's hard to wrap our minds around because it could require a one-hundred-eighty-degree shift in our thinking. That single verse challenged my long-held perspective that death was a thing to be dreaded and feared.

The thought of our own death is hard enough to think about, but if you're like me, the death of those I love is so much harder.

If my son had died during his code blue episode or at one of the many other times I was told he would, would I have really believed that day to be better than that of his birth? Think of the countless people you have loved and lost. Did you feel their day of death to be better than their day of birth?

"The day of our death, which will put a period to our cares, and toils, and sorrows, and remove us to rest, and joy, and eternal satisfaction, is better than the day of our birth, which ushered us into a world of so much sin and trouble, vanity and vexation. The day of our birth clogged our souls with the burden of the flesh, but the day of our death will set them at liberty from that burden," Matthew Henry said of this verse in Ecclesiastes. This kind of mindset requires a wisdom that cannot come except by the Holy Spirit of the living God, who is infinitely wiser that we are, granting it to us.

Have you ever noticed that long before a newborn enters the world, the day of their birth has been wildly talked about, anticipated, imagined, and meticulously prepared for? Why? For one, the excitement and anticipation calls for it. Mothers especially wonder what the new life growing inside them will be like and what kind of mother they'll be. Secondly, and most importantly, that day requires a great deal of preparation. How will the baby be born? Where? Will the mother breastfeed or use formula? What will the baby's name be? Are there enough diapers, bottles, wipes, and burp clothes? What will they wear home from the hospital? Has the home been prepared for the arrival of a baby? Will dad need to take time off work to help mom? The list goes on and on.

Obviously, great preparation and discussion go on about the day of one's birth, but not so much about the day of one's death—even though the Bible says it's a better day. I realize this may be challenging your thinking just as mine has been challenged. A statement like that takes time to digest. The matter of death is not an easy one to think about; that's part of why this book is a devotional. We may need to chew on it in little bits. That's okay too. Better a little to be taken to heart and absorbed than a lot that will come to nothing.

"Precious in the sight of the Lord is the death of his saints" (Ps. 116:15 KJV).

"For to me to live is Christ, and to die is gain" (Phil. 1:21 KJV).

We see three other words accompany *death*, *die*, and *dying* in scripture: *better*, *precious*, and *gain*. Three words that, I must confess, I don't always think of first when death comes to my mind.

Of course, death is a time of grief, but we do not have to sorrow as others who have no hope (1 Thess. 4:13). Death does not have to be feared and can even be an acceptable topic of discussion. Throughout this book, I hope to challenge our thinking and show that not only can it be, but it *should* be.

As Charles Spurgeon said in his sermon, The House of Mourning and the House of Feasting, "So, we ought often to accustom our souls to the thought of death, to make death a familiar thing, to talk with it every day."

Called to Action

Ask:

Am I comfortable talking about death?

If not, what makes me uncomfortable about it?

Continue Asking:

God, what do you want me to do before I die?

LAY IT TO HEART

It is better to go to the house of mourning,
than to go to the house of feasting: for that is
the end of all men; and the living will lay it to
his heart.
—Ecclesiastes 7:2 KJV

That is best for us which is best for our souls,
by which the heart is made better, though it
be unpleasing to sense.
—Matthew Henry

King Solomon didn't end his discourse with the conclusion that the day of one's death is better than their birth. He was merely setting the stage.

"It is better to go to the house of mourning, than to the house of feasting: for that is the end of all men; and the living will lay it to his heart" (Eccles. 7:2 KJV).

Wisdom drips like honey in this verse. Let's look at what the house of mourning is. In the original language, *mourning* is meant as a wail, or cry, for the dead. In today's usage, it is simply a funeral. The house of feasting, on the other hand, is a banquet; a time of drinking. Who on earth would rather be at a funeral than at a celebration?

In speaking of this verse in his sermon, The House of Mourning and the House of Feasting, Charles Spurgeon said, "It is better to go to the house of mourning. God has said it, so let not unbelief deny what God positively declares. Unto all of you who know not how soon any one of you may be there, I speak in the name of the Lord and I say, go to the house of mourning. If you get an invitation to a wedding and an invitation to a funeral, lay the funeral note on the top! Do not disdain to go there, O child of God, for the Holy Spirit will so reveal Jesus by the bedside of the mourner."

Matthew Henry's commentary of this verse says , "It is better to go to the house of mourning, and there weep with those that weep, than to go to the house of feasting, to a wedding, or a wake, there to rejoice with those that do rejoice. It will do us more good, and make better impressions upon us. It is better for us to go to the house of mourning, not to see the pomp of the funeral, but to share in the sorrow of it, and to learn good lessons, both from the dead, who is going thence to his long home, and from the mourners, who go about the streets."

Lessons are learned in the house of mourning that cannot be learned elsewhere. Where have you thought more of your own mortality than at a funeral? As this verse states, the house of mourning will come to all men. When have you had more compassion upon others than when you have watched them grieve?

The latter part of this verse is where you and I are now: "...the living will lay it to his heart."

We who are alive are to apply this truth to our hearts. Matthew Henry wisely commented on this truth in his commentary of verse two in Ecclesiastes chapter seven when he said, "'The living will lay it to his heart.' Will they? It were well if they would. Those that are spiritually alive will lay it to heart, and, as for all the survivors, one would think they should; it is their own fault if they do not, for nothing is more easy and natural than by the death of others to be put in mind of our own."

Called to Action

Ask:

Have I spent more time in my life in the house of feasting than in the house of mourning?

Have I laid to heart that the house of feasting is better for my soul and the good of those around me?

Make a list observing thoughts or reflections you've had while at a funeral. If you haven't been to one, remember this as you attend one in the future. Compare your thoughts to those you've had while celebrating.

Continue Asking:

God, what do you want me to do before I die?

WHAT TIME IS IT?

*...ye can discern the face of the sky; but can ye
not discern the signs of the times?*
—Matthew 16:3 KJV

*Lord, do not allow any of us to be blind to the
heavenly signs, — thy cross, thy resurrection,
thy Word, thy Spirit, and thy work of grace...*
—Charles Spurgeon

"Something's not right," I told the doctor.

Leading up to the illness that nearly killed my son, there were signs. Somewhere along the way, his healthy pink skin turned an eerie shade of green. He had trouble breathing and, one epic night, had to be resuscitated seventeen times. His blood culture returned positive as sepsis crept into his bloodstream. When liver failure approached, I didn't know what was happening, but I knew it was something serious. There were signs. I can't explain how I knew because I'd never seen a deathly ill baby before, but deep down I knew.

In the months and years that followed the trauma of my twins premature birth and subsequent hospitalization, my heart didn't escape unscathed. I'd professed to know Christ for thirty-two years but trials and adversity had a way of exposing the best of my professions. In those months of 2011 that led up to the darkest days of my life, there were signs of impending implosion.

There were signs of my hypocrisy despite a thirty-two-year pro-
fession of Christianity. Sadly, I ignored them. Numbness felt better than pain. If only I could go back and right wrongs. If only I
had heeded the signs.

Signs of the times have always been present. In Matthew 24,
on the Mount of Olives, Jesus went into great detail about them
to his disciples. In 2 Timothy, even more signs of the last days
are listed.

> *"But know this: hard times will come in the last days.
> For people will be lovers of self, lovers of money,
> boastful, proud, demeaning , disobedient to parents,
> ungrateful, unholy, unloving, irreconcilable, slan-
> derers, without self-control, brutal, without love for
> what is good, traitors, reckless, conceited, lovers of
> pleasure rather than lovers of God, holding to the
> form of godliness but denying its power"* (2 Tim.
> 3:1-5 CSB).

I've never seen a more blatant, unapologetic display of this list
than I do now—and I imagine the generations before me would
echo my sentiment.

"Learn this lesson from the fig tree," Jesus said. "As soon as its
branch becomes tender and sprouts leaves, you know that summer is near. In the same way, when you see all these things, recognize that he is near—at the door" (Matt. 24:32-33 CSB).

While I am not an expert on eschatology, I do see the signs
surrounding me and I believe the return of our Savior is immi-
nent. I believe he is even at the door. Do you hear his footsteps?
Is he knocking at the door of your heart?

Our nation and our hearts are both in crisis. Jesus is the rem-
edy. Dear brother and sister, if we believe this truth, mustn't we
prepare for his return? Mustn't we deeply concern ourselves

with the very things he put us on the earth to accomplish; to be about his work, for we know not what time remains.

"Oh, children of God," said Charles Spurgeon in his sermon, Signs of the Times, "I pray you discern the times before the threatening shower descends upon our country, and learn to play your parts as men of God, ordained to defend the truth. What is your duty at the present crisis?"

What a question. If phrased another way, wasn't he asking the same thing we are? What is our duty before we die?

Dear One, as signs indicate the times around us, they also reflect what is within us. Is the unresolved anger, bitterness, or resentment in your heart a sign of the unforgiveness you're harboring? Do words of judgment flow freer than words of compassion? When you're faced with a difficult decision, do you pray before making it? When you tell others you'll be praying for them, do you?

What are the signs around you saying? What are they saying within you?

Called to Action

Ask:

What is my duty during the present crisis in my life, my home, my job, my relationships, my country?

Continue Asking:

God, what do you want me to do before I die?

REDEEMING THE TIME

*See then that ye walk circumspectly, not
as fools, but as wise, redeeming the time,
because the days are evil.*
—Ephesians 5:15-16 KJV

*It is a great part of Christian wisdom to
redeem the time. They should make the best
use they can of the present seasons of grace.*
—Matthew Henry

"That's an hour of my life I'll never get back."

It's a popular phrase we say in jest, but have we ever stopped to think about what we've said? Basically, that what we just did was a complete and utter waste of our time. A quick glance into my past would have me saying that, not just of hours and days, but even of entire months.

Most of us have heard the saying "living on borrowed time," and while it's often used to describe someone who, like my son, was told he would die but hasn't, isn't all time really borrowed? We don't own it. There is no pause, fast-forward, or rewind button we can hit.

Scripture instructs us to do something interesting with time: "See then that ye walk circumspectly, not as fools, but as wise, redeeming the time, because the days are evil" (Eph. 5:16 KJV).

The original Greek word for redeem means to rescue from loss; to make a wise and sacred use of every opportunity for doing good.

The CSB translation of this verse lays out its meaning well: "Pay careful attention, then, to how you live—not as unwise people but as wise, making the most of the time, because the days are evil."

The phrase that stands out to me is from the Greek translation : "to rescue from loss." As strands of long brown hair turn gray, the mirror reminds me of the time I'm losing. I never realized how quickly time could pass until I raised my children.

"You better enjoy it now. It'll be gone before you know it. The days are long, honey, but the years are short."

Over the years, countless gray-haired mothers have gone out of their way at grocery stores to tell me this. Compelled to walk up to a complete stranger, they wanted me to understand the truth in Ephesians—that we are continually losing time and it must be rescued. It must be captured and seized. With their children long since out of their homes, pangs of loneliness no doubt propelled their comments.

In his commentary on Ephesians 5:15-16, Charles Spurgeon said, "Buying up the hours; they are of such value that you cannot pay too high a price for them."

I fear I have grossly undervalued time in my life. I fear I have not paid a high enough price for the hours. Oh, the moments I have grieved once gone. Oh, the moments right in front of me I have missed.

If that is you too, Friend, don't lose heart. While we don't own time, we have all been given charge over a measure of it. An undetermined portion has been dropped in our laps. Though little by little it slips from our grasp, today, this very minute, let's take charge of the moments we have. Let's buy them back. Let's redeem them and make every minute count.

Called to Action

Ask:

Have I undervalued time in my life? Have I not been willing to pay a high enough price for the hours?

What do I have to show for the time I've been given? What do I want it to look like?

Dear God, what is one simple step I can make, this very hour, toward making wise use of the time you've given me?

Continue Asking:

What do you want me to do before I die, God?

A TIME TO EVERY PURPOSE

*To everything there is a season, and a time to
every purpose under the heaven.*
—Ecclesiastes 3:1 KJV

*We are not long in any one state and we
quickly change from one condition to
another.*
—Charles Spurgeon

Glancing out your window, you notice that spring's vibrant tulips have wilted. Before you could enjoy the season or the flowers, suddenly they're gone. Summer's brutal heat soon replaces them both. Out of nowhere, autumn rushes in like a tidal wave—but charges out just again as quickly. Winter's bitter cold meets it and hangs around like an unwelcomed guest. Creatively and intelligently designed, earth was made to move and change as it rotates around the sun. Nothing we do will alter that plan.

Ecclesiastes, the famous book of wisdom literature, says there is a time for everything, including "a time to be born, and a time to die." We can no more change this than we can change earth's composition or alter its seasons. They just are and must be accepted whether we like them or not.

"Seed-time and harvest, summer and winter, have come according to his word without our aid, and, wonderful as these changes are, they have never failed," said Charles Spurgeon in his sermon entitled, The Sermon of the Seasons.

In his commentary, Matthew Henry said, "These are determined by the divine counsel; and, as we were born, so we must die, at the time appointed."

Ecclesiastes goes on to say there is a time to/for:

- plant and pluck up
- kill and heal
- break down and build up
- weep and laugh
- mourn and dance
- cast away stones and gather them
- embrace and refrain from embracing
- get and lose
- keep and cast away
- rend and sew
- keep silent and speak
- love and hate
- war and peace.

The longer we live, the more we see these times realized in our lives. At two o'clock in the morning on December 10, 2007, I became aware of how dangerously close these times are to each other when my water broke only thirty weeks into my picture-perfect pregnancy with twin boys. At bedtime I was laughing; within a matter of hours, I was weeping.

Every season serves a purpose. Few know this as well as farmers, whose job it is to study and know the seasons. Their livelihoods depend upon their knowledge of the times of planting and harvesting and I daresay, fellow believer, so do ours.

Sometimes we need to dance but sometimes we need to mourn. Sometimes we need to keep but sometimes we need to give. Sometimes we need to sew but sometimes we need to rend.

As Matthew Henry observed in his commentary of Ecclesiastes chapter three, "There is a time for men to plant, a time of the year, a time of their lives; but, when that which was planted has grown fruitless and useless, it is time to pluck it up."

Called to Action

Ask:

What season am I in?

Has what's been planted in my life grown fruitless and useless?

What needs to be plucked up?

Have I kept things or people in my life that I need to let go of?

Have I allowed them to keep me from living my purpose?

Have I tried to patch up the broken pieces of my heart when I need to rend them before God?

Continue Asking:

What do you want me to do before I die, God?

IN THE MEANTIME

Wait on the Lord: be of good courage, and he shall strengthen thine heart: wait, I say, on the Lord.
—Psalm 27:14 KJV

Keep close to God and to your duty.
—Matthew Henry

"Your son will spend nearly his first year of life in two hospitals."

If someone had told me that on our first day in the NICU, I wouldn't have believed them, nor could I have handled that kind of information. Throughout those three hundred and twenty-four days there were times of bustling activity and times we stood at death's door, but most often, there were times of waiting.

There were hours of waiting to see if surgeries would be successful. There were months of waiting to see if the experimental drug we'd flown over a thousand miles to try would actually work. After returning home from the hospital, there were years of waiting to see if my son would be as brain damaged as doctors said he would be. In the waiting, sounds of doting grandparents were replaced with beeping monitors. Moments of bonding were replaced with a gentle rub through the hole of an isolette upon the frail arms of babies so small they appeared more like little birds. In the waiting, the voices in my head screamed.

It wasn't supposed to be this way.

Sometimes we know we're right where we're meant to be. We're content to see no further. At other times in our lives, we know there's more. We've seen and felt it in prayer. It's beginning to take shape but we're still not ready yet. I wanted my twins to be well and to be well now. I wanted to unhook them from their monitors and bring them home right then, but if I had done that the consequences would have been dire. It wasn't time yet.

Rebekah, a former neighbor, godly mother of eight children, and my dear friend, reminds me frequently that God's calling often feels like pregnancy. Once you know the baby is coming there's still a period of waiting. Our bodies, minds, and hearts are all going through a time of preparation, and waiting is not optional.

When God births a dream or calling inside of us, what do we do in the meantime? When we're waiting for a dream or calling to be made known inside of us, what do we do while we wait?

More likely than not, you will experience many times of waiting too. Sometimes it seems the wait will never end, but it will. The fact that you are holding this book in your hands and reading it is evidence of that. A far surer evidence, though, is that God's word promises that if we wait on the Lord and are of good courage, he will strengthen our hearts.

In the meantime, trust that. Trust that there is a purpose in the waiting.

Called to Action

Ask:

Has the Holy Spirit revealed a dream or calling in my life that I am to pursue? If I'm pursuing it, how am I holding up in the meantime?

Am I waiting to realize God's will and purpose for my life? How am I holding up in the meantime?

Asking hard questions is an important step. Let's take another and begin to search for the answers. In almost every situation in life, if we don't know the answer to a question, what do we do? We ask; we go to someone who knows. In this book, we're asking ourselves and, more importantly, we're asking God.

Proverbs 2:3-5 says, "Furthermore, if you call out to insight and lift your voice to understanding, if you seek it like silver and search for it like hidden treasure, then you will understand the fear of the Lord and discover the knowledge of God."

Continue Asking:

What do you want me to do before I die, God?

IN DUE TIME

*And let us not be weary in well doing: for in
due season we shall reap, if we faint not.*
—Galatians 6:9 KJV

*As we should not excuse ourselves from any
part of our duty, so neither should we grow
weary in it.*
—Matthew Henry

W e're admonished in Galatians 6:9 to stay the course and not grow weary, but I must tell you, I grew weary in the waiting. I got tired of hearing the incessant beeping of monitors. I was exasperated by the platitudes offered by well-meaning onlookers who had no idea the realities I faced. In the meantime, I struggled immensely.

For years I knew God's call on my life was in part to write, but I didn't really know exactly what that looked like. With every opportunity that presented itself, I continued writing, continued seeking. The wait was hard, especially when those around me seemed to be stepping into their callings with such ease. But that was their time. Mine was not yet.

In the original Greek language, the meaning of the word translated above as *due* is interesting.

Idios: pertaining to oneself, one's own. Used universally, of what is one's own as opposed to belonging to another.

The Greek word for season, *kairos*, means a fixed or definite time.

We can break this down to mean simply *your time*. Your time—not someone else's. To go back to my friend's analogy of childbirth, think about what we say to a woman who is pregnant. When are *you due*? In other words, when is *your time*?

Sometimes seeing someone else's time arrive can be hard. It can cause envy. That envy can feed on our insecurities and we can be tempted to either doubt our calling or give up hope that our due time will ever come.

Charles Spurgeon, in his commentary on Galatians 6:9, said of the word *weary*, "I find the Greek word contains the idea of being disheartened. Let us not lose heart. This is a soul-weariness against which we must resolutely fight. It comes to many good workers and shows itself in different ways. Some think the work less important than they did at first. Others fear that their part of it will prove an utter failure. This is heart-weariness."

Your due time will come if you do not faint, Friend. How do I know that? Because God's word promises it will: "...for in due season we shall reap, if we faint not."

Called to Action

Ask:

Is my heart weary as I wait for my due time?

Do I compare my life with others and grow discontented when their time comes?

Does fear of failing keep me weary?

Continue Asking:

What do you want me to do before I die, God?

NOW THE TIME IS

*And that, knowing the time, that now it is
high time to awake out of sleep: for now, is
our salvation nearer than when we believed.*
—Romans 13:11 KJV

*...the only time I have is that which is just
now passing. Did I say I had it? While I said I
had it, it is gone...*
—Charles Spurgeon

"**G**et anyone you ever want to see your son and get them here *now!*"

There was an immediacy in the neonatologist's inflection and his meaning was crystal clear.

"Mom, come here *now!*"

Over the years, my children have echoed those words after a bad fall, a deep cut, or when they were convinced monsters lived in their closets.

"Code blue. Pod A—room two. I repeat, code blue. Pod A—room two. All medical staff report, *stat!*"

The word *now* seems to need no further study, but there's something about seeing its meaning in black and white that makes me ponder its connotation more deeply. Nearly every dictionary I grabbed (I won't admit to how many I have) listed its meaning as "at the present time or moment." Dictionary.com added to that meaning, "without further delay; immediately; at once."

Derived from the Latin word *statim*, stat has an identical meaning: "immediately, at once."

In light of these meanings, let's look again at our verse.

"...*now* (at once; immediately) it is high time to awake out of sleep..."

Not tomorrow—at once. Not next month or next year—immediately. We've heard that ignorance is bliss, but the truth is, ignorance is just plain ignorance; in the end, it is really our enemy, not our friend. Sleeping may feel better than being awake at times, but little work gets done when we're sleeping.

In his sermon entitled "Now," Charles Spurgeon said, "Now is the time to wake from our sleep, beloved. My brother, I do not care what you mean to do tomorrow, but I do care about what you intend to do today. Oh! Those day-dreams of ours! We are always intending in a year or two's time to be such valorous defenders of the faith, such good soldiers of Christ, such good winners of souls. My dear brother, what art thou doing now?"

Spurgeon went on to say, "The great mischief of the most of men is that they procrastinate."

I seem to have come wired with only two gears: now and later. Oh, the mischief my procrastination has caused me over the years. Often, I put off and put off until what I dreaded becomes unavoidable. What I inevitably learn in most cases is that my dread of the thing was far worse than the thing itself. What I fretted over could have been done and my worry ceased had I but exchanged the put-off for the now.

This mentality is especially dangerous for the Christian because procrastination is very presumptuous. Procrastination says tomorrow will come and I will put it off until then.

I'll apologize later.
I'll visit my parents later.

I'll exercise later.
I'll get my heart right later.
I'll repent later.

Now the time is, as scripture says, because now is present tense when all other time is either past or future. Precious saint, what are you doing now? Now is guaranteed. Now, we can make the phone calls we've needed to make for a very long time. Now, we can visit someone we've put off visiting. Now we can pick up our Bibles and read. Most importantly, now we can drop to our knees and surrender our hearts and lives to the call God has placed upon them.

It's okay not to know what that call is. It's okay for it to be exactly what we're doing right now. It's okay for it to be a dream we're still waiting to happen. The important thing is that now, this very minute, we are pursuing it with all that is within us.

Called to Action

Ask:

Have I buried my head in the sand to avoid realities I need to face in my life? Some you may know and some you may not. Ask God to expose these areas in your life.

Have I allowed fear and insecurity to keep me from action? Make a list of the areas you've allowed this to happen. Go back to the blank space at the beginning and write them. Keep them before you and be on guard against them.

Today, right now, I need to face _____.

Continue Asking:

Fear and insecurity go hand in hand because in reality, insecurity is fear. I've been held captive by them at times in my life and I'm sure you have too. Until they are dealt with and overcome, they could keep us from asking the question we all need to ask:

What do you want me to do before I die, God?

NEVER TOO EARLY, NEVER TOO LATE

*Wisdom is found with the elderly, and
understanding comes with long life.*
—Job 12:12 CSB

*The soul's price does not depend upon its
years.*
—Charles Spurgeon

"**A**nd the winner goes to..."

A name I didn't recognize followed the announcement made by the host at my first writer's conference. A hush fell over the crowd as we all waited for the winner to claim their award. The stage sat empty for the longest time before, out of the corner of my eye, I saw an elderly woman approach the steps. She took her sweet time climbing and slowly strolled across the stage with as much confidence as a beauty queen awaiting her crown. Clasping the microphone with worn and shaky hands, she announced, "I'm eighty-four years old and I want to say thank you."

Eighty-four. Let that sink in a minute.

At eighty-four, her words were no less important than another's words. This award-winning author's words had no less of an impact at age eighty-four and her calling was no less sure than yours or mine.

Can you imagine how many battles she must have fought in eight-four years? Countless doubts must have filled her mind and yet she did something many never do: She overcame them and dared—at her age, as many would say—to *go*.

How many lives had her words already touched? How many will they affect long after she travels beyond the veil? Both the beauty and the importance of words is that though the author ages, they do not. Words transcend time.

I believe God's callings do too, "for the gifts and calling of God are without repentance" (Rom. 11:29).

"Mom, can I go tell them what Jesus did for me?"

Isaiah, my five-year-old son, asked me this after returning to the table at Cracker Barrel one morning. His father and brothers were still in the restroom, but he'd finished and darted back to his chocolate milk. I watched him drinking through a straw with tears in my eyes, remembering the years he'd been fed through a feeding tube and unable to drink at all.

"Sure," I said as I glanced over to the table next to us. Unaware they were about to be ambushed, a couple likely in their fifties sat across from a young man who appeared to be in his mid-twenties.

"Come with me, Mom." My son's boldness surprised me. Wanting to ensure his safety, I walked beside him.

Once at the edge of the strangers' table, he lifted his shirt to expose his scarred abdomen.

"Hi, my name is Isaiah. I was born very early. I had thirteen surgeries and I was supposed to die but Jesus saved my life."

Tears flowed from the woman's eyes, as she brought her hands to her face to cover the sobs. Her husband's glasses shielded tears he couldn't keep in as the young man across from them scooted his chair back and raised his own shirt.

"I was born very early and I was supposed to die too," he said.

A scar that stretched nearly the length and width of his chest peeked from beneath his shirt. He went on to tell us that he'd also been born a micro-preemie and had open-heart surgery.

I was at a loss for words, but as our eyes met, we knew they weren't necessary. The words of my young son had just crossed barriers he seemed too young to cross. Never had I been more aware that God can use the tiniest of willing hearts to do his work.

Perhaps you feel too young or that it's too early. Perhaps you feel too old; that it's too late. May the words of Charles Spurgeon from his devotion book entitled, Morning and Evening, be as ointment for your soul.

"You may fear that the Lord has passed you by, but it is not so: He who counts the stars, and calls them by their names, is in no danger of forgetting His own children. He knows your case as thoroughly as if you were the only creature He ever made, or the only saint He ever loved. Approach Him and be at peace."

Called to Action

Ask:

How are the lies stacking up? Have I believed those that say, "I'm too old" or "I'm too young"?

If I continue believing that, how will I ever reach my greatest potential for usefulness?

Right now, let's leave the past in the past. What's done is done and what's not done is not done. But you are here in this moment, and right now you can be useful in so many beautiful ways. Whether old or young, write down one useful thing you've done today.

Today I Started writing an outline for my memoir. (or whatever it's supposed to be)

Continue Asking:

God, what do you want me to do before I die?

WHAT'S IN THE BUCKET

*But lay up for yourselves treasures in heaven,
where neither moth nor rust doth corrupt,
and where thieves do not break through nor
steal.*
—Matthew 6:20 KJV

*The promises are bills of exchange, by which
all true believers return their treasure to
heaven, payable in the future state: and thus
we make that sure that will be made sure.*
—Matthew Henry

*B*ucket list: a list of things that one has not done before but wants to do before dying.

Two hundred and ninety-six million results came up when I typed the words *bucket list* into a Google search. Clearly, there is no shortage of ideas on what to do before we die—or of people in search of those ideas. In one way or another, aren't we all searching for meaning and purpose? Most of us want to make an impact, we just don't always know how.

Whether we realize it or not and whether we intend to or not, we are filling our buckets every day. What exactly are we filling them with? Scripture instructs us to lay up for ourselves treasures in heaven which cannot be stolen or destroyed. In his commentary on this verse, Matthew Henry said, "It concerns thee to choose wisely, for thou art choosing for thyself, and shalt have as thou choosest."

Ouch.

That seems harsh but I know I needed to hear it. I've made so many choices that I would give almost anything to go back and change.

I'm not at all suggesting we should kick the bucket and let its contents spill out as if our efforts to fill it have been futile or pointless. What I am suggesting is that we closely examine what's in our buckets. In light of Matthew 6:20, how do the contents hold up? What are we treasuring, and do we really want to store it? What really matters to you? Are those things in your bucket?

The beauty of storing up treasures in heaven is the implication and promise of future enjoyment. Notice whom the verse says the treasures are for: They are for you. That's wonderful news, but also notice where the treasures are. Your treasures are in Heaven. When I get a little too comfortable and want to start opening treasures, I have to remind myself that I'm not there and it's just not time yet.

I see this in my children continually. Daily, I have to remind my teenage and tween sons that I need them to take care of their responsibilities before they can play a game, invite a friend over, or explore the woods. I want them to enjoy the games, their friends, and the woods, but I need their help first.

According to Matthew Henry's commentary, "it is a great encouragement to us to lay up our treasure in heaven, that there it is safe; it will not decay of itself, no moth nor rust will corrupt it; nor can we be by force or fraud deprived of it; thieves do not break through and steal. It is a happiness above and beyond the changes and chances of time, an inheritance incorruptible."

Many people are racing to fill their buckets here on earth without realizing there are treasures in store for us beyond the veil. I don't believe the believer's bucket ends at death. In fact, I'm making a list of things I want to do after I die, as well as before. I want to hug Mary, mother to mother, and tell her I'm so sorry she had to witness the brutal death of her son. I'd love to have a yearlong conversation with the likes of Paul, Peter, and John. I'd like to thank Charles Spurgeon and Matthew Henry for their lifelong studies of God's word and for their tireless commitment to dig for treasures in the Bible and share them with the world. Most of all, I want to run with arms open wide toward my Savior. I want to hold him the way he held me in his heart on the cross. I want to thank him for rescuing this wretched sinner from a life of pain, misery, and aimless wandering.

What a joy it would be to fulfill my husband's lifelong dream and take him and our boys on a trip to Ireland. I don't fret because that will likely never happen here. The God who spoke the world into existence and created such indescribable beauty knows how much our hearts desire it, and I have every confidence that whether in this life or the next, he will let us see it.

Buckets are great. They are meant to be filled and I would say that having a bucket is better than not having one at all. I urge us, however, to see to it that the treasures we seek to store are right where they should be. There will be no greater return on any investments we will ever make than the ones we make in heaven.

Called to Action

Ask:

What's in my bucket?

What do I treasure?

Are my treasures on earth or in heaven?

Continue Asking:

What do you want me to do before I die, God?

CHOSEN

*According as he hath chosen us in him before
the foundation of the world...*
—Ephesians 1:4-6 KJV

*It's a good thing God chose me before I was
born, because He surely would not have
afterwards.*
—Charles Spurgeon

A self-admitted blasphemer and chief of sinners, if anyone might have felt they'd gone too far to be used by God, I'd say it was Paul.

- He consented to the stoning of Stephen, the first Christian martyr.
- He searched for Christians house by house and hauled them to prison.
- He spoke of slaughter and threatened the disciples of the Lord.
- He persecuted Christ.

In spite of all that, a blindingly divine appointment awaited him on the road to Damascus one extraordinary day. His radical conversion to Christianity is perhaps one of the most talked about in history. As it turns out, he had been chosen to bear Christ's name before the Gentiles.

A persecutor, chosen? A blasphemer, chosen?

Following Paul's conversion, Jesus instructed Ananias to lay his hands on Paul's eyes so he could see again. According to Acts 9:18, when he did, "immediately there fell from [Paul's] eyes as it had been scales and he received sight, arose and was baptized."

A brief glimpse into my own past reminds me of Saul. The road I walked along was tinged pink from the rose-colored glasses I wore. I thought I was on the right road to happiness. Sadly, up to that point, I suppose that was my purpose. I thought I was doing all the right things. I imagine Paul thought he was too, but after his encounter with Christ, Saul became Paul—he was radically changed. On February 14, 2011, so was I. God confronted me along my journey and exposed my heart. The scales that covered Paul's eyes fell. In the most miraculous way, my rose-colored glasses shattered and for the first time in my life I could truly see.

Acts 9 tells us that Paul stayed with the disciples for several days following his encounter. Then the Bible says he does something very noteworthy: He "straightway" preached Christ in the synagogues. In spite of his past and having gone from Christ-hater to Christ-advocate in a matter of days, Paul wasted no time getting to the work he had been called to do. A great deal could be learned from this one verse.

Imagine for a moment Paul having doubts like us, feelings of inadequacy to the point he felt God could no longer use a man like him. What if he had wallowed in that and allowed his insecurities to immobilize him? What would church history look life if he had? How much smaller would our Bibles be without Paul?

What, Precious Saint, could the future look like without your obedience?

What could it look like with it? Let us never underestimate the power of God to use the lowest of the low, the vilest of people or the dirtiest of all sinners. Isn't that exactly who he came to use?

I have little doubt that Paul's past contributed immensely to his future. His determination to follow Christ was evident in the level of passion and commitment he showed. His feelings of unworthiness over the gift of mercy Christ showed him no doubt fueled his ministry. I imagine Paul's thoughts joining my own.

If Christ can save me, he can save anyone. If he can use me, he can use anyone.

If that's you, let Paul's story remind you that Christ can, and he will.

As Ephesians 1:4-6 KJV states, "According as he hath chosen us in him before the foundation of the world, that we should be holy and without blame before him in love; having predestinated us unto the adoption of children by Jesus Christ to himself, according to the good pleasure of his will, to the praise of the glory of his grace, wherein he hath made us accepted in the beloved."

Called to Action

Ask:

Have I believed the lie that because of my past, God can no longer use me?

Continue Asking:

God, what do you want me to do before I die?

If you weren't sure when you began reading, has something become clear? Have you had thoughts or ideas as you've been seeking God that you need to write down? Write them here. Hopefully, you can watch them unfold as you read this book.

Before I die, God wants me to:

DAY TWENTY-ONE

BETTER THAN A DEAD LION

For to him that is joined to all the living there is hope; for a living dog is better than a dead lion.
—Ecclesiastes 9:4 KJV

Dum spiro, spero.
(Latin: While I breathe, I hope.)

Most structures look sturdy from the outside, but until a storm comes along, breaks down the walls, and exposes the foundation, you don't really know what lies underneath. When my twin sons were born premature, in a matter of minutes, my picture-perfect rug was jerked out from under me.

At three pounds and several ounces, Joshua had a single operation, spent two months in the NICU, and came home with a feeding tube. His twin, Isaiah, weighed three pounds and had a very different journey. He spent several days shy of his first eleven months in two NICUs, endured thirteen operations, went into liver failure, was transported 1,100 miles away to Boston, Massachusetts to be in a clinical trial—and that's just scratching the surface.

"Your son is the sickest baby in the entire hospital right now."

"If it is what I think it is, your son has twelve to twenty-four hours to live."

"Get anyone you ever want to see this baby to the hospital now."

Those were just a few of the many phrases my husband and I were told during our son's nearly year-long hospital stay. During that excruciatingly painful time in my life and for thirty-two years prior, I'd professed to know Christ, but as the days turned into months and the flames got hotter, God exposed the true condition of my heart. It was darker than I'd ever realized.

As detailed in my memoir, life's rose-colored glasses shattered. One dreadfully beautiful day, the house I was convinced I'd built to stand upon the rock sunk in the sand. In a profound way, I came face-to-face with the darkness of my own heart. In a crumpled heap on my bedroom floor, I had been exposed for the hypocrite I was.

You've gone too far.

That thought permeated my mind as I lay before Christ, fully exposed. For years that fear gripped my heart.

You've blown it. God will never use you now.

An ambitious go-getter who never backed down at the thought of an exciting new challenge, opportunity, or job since I was a little girl, all I'd ever really wanted to do was please God and encourage others. Always the dreamer, I'd imagined the great and wonderful things I might do for him, but I was now convinced those could no longer be.

That was one of the biggest lies on my list and I believed it wholeheartedly until I began noticing that there were some really interesting characters in the Bible who underwent colossal failures. As I read, I noticed an interesting pattern unfold. Those people were the exact ones God often used. In story after redemptive story, God used the broken, battered people and their failures. That meant there was hope for me and there's hope for you, too.

"For to him that is joined to all the living there is hope; for a living dog is better than a dead lion" (Eccles. 9:4 KJV).

We're joined to all the living because we're alive right now. The Bible says, "there is hope." What three words could be better than that?

There is hope.

A lion seems far superior to a dog, except in the case of a dead one. A living dog, scripture says, is better than a dead lion. Why? Because the living dog is alive and therefore has hope.

In his commentary of Ecclesiastes 9:4, Charles Spurgeon says, "If the heart be full of evil, and madness be in it, yet while there is life there is hope that by the grace of God there may be a blessed change wrought; but after men go to the dead it is too late then; he that is then filthy will be filthy still, forever filthy. If men be thrown aside as useless, yet, while they are joined to the living, there is hope that they may yet again take root and bear fruit; he that is alive is, or may be, good for something, but he that is dead, as to this world, is not capable of being any further serviceable. Therefore, a living dog is better than a dead lion."

No matter what lies in your past, there is hope for you too, Dear One. I know this because you wouldn't be holding this book if it were untrue. If you've been believing the lie, like I did, that you've gone too far or that God can never use you now, write it down and take it to God. Pore through the stacks of Bible stories that prove us wrong.

- Moses killed a man.
- Jonah refused to obey God and go to Nineveh.
- David committed adultery and had a man killed.
- Paul persecuted Christians.
- The sinful woman's sins were many.
- Peter denied Jesus three times, and on the list goes.

If God can use them, he can use you. He can and he will.

Called to Action

Ask:

Do I believe that I've gone too far to be used by God? Is that true?

Do I see from scripture that God uses broken people?

Has this lie kept me from fulfilling God's call on my life?

Continue Asking:

What do you want me to do before I die, God?

DAY TWENTY-TWO

WHICH SON ARE YOU?

Son, go work today in my vineyard.
—Matthew 21:28 KJV

The gospel call to work in the vineyard, requires present obedience; Son, go work to-day, while it is called to-day, because the night comes when no man can work. We were not sent into the world to be idle, nor had we daylight given us to play by; and therefore, if ever we mean to do anything for God and our souls, why not now? Why not to-day?
—Matthew Henry

"What do you think? A man had two sons. He went to the first and said, "My son, go work in the vineyard today. The son answered, "I don't want to," but later he changed his mind and went. Then the man went to the other and said the same thing. "I will, sir," he answered, but he didn't go. Which of the two did his father's will? (Matt. 21:28-31 CSB)

"Mom, will you color with me?" Your daughter's request doesn't go unnoticed, but you're just too busy.

"I'm sorry honey. I can't right now."

You try to continue working, but her sweet voice rings in your ear until it merges with the guilt you feel.

"You know what, I'm so sorry. I'm never too busy to spend time with you, sweetheart. Pass me the crayons." This mother and the first son have a lot in common.

"Dad, will you play catch with me?"

"Yes, of course I will, Son. I'll meet you outside." Before heading out your phone rings and you never make it out the door.

Both of these parents love their children deeply, but what separates the two? When asked to do something important, one said she couldn't. Later, she apologized and ultimately did what she was asked to do. The other, after being asked, immediately and likely enthusiastically answered, "Yes, of course," but never went. His follow-through fell short of his declaration.

This is just one of many possible examples of what's happening with the two sons in Jesus's parable from Matthew. I've been both of these parents at various times over the years. Unfortunately, I've been both of them as a spouse, a sibling, and an employee as well.

Did you happen to notice the question Jesus asked at the beginning of his parable?

What do you think?

Jesus wanted his disciples to think about what he was going to say because it was profoundly important. His initial question was followed by an important command, "My son, go work today in my vineyard."

A clear and direct command was given by the father to the sons. A father's commands are not optional. They are not subject to feelings or whatever else may be on the to-do list at the time. There was work to be done and the father needed his sons to do it.

We haven't quite gotten to the lesson of the parable yet, but I need to stop right here for a moment. I need to ask myself a tough question first.

Am I even working in my Father's vineyard at all?

As I examine the two sons, it seems clear that they both have issues. Neither seems to be the model child because neither of them does what they say they will do. When told to go work, the first son immediately says no, but later changes his mind and goes. The other says he'll go, but never goes at all.

How many times have we been asked to do something and our initial response was "Yes," but we never did it? Like the father who promised his son he would play catch but never went, our words without action are in vain.

Jesus goes on to ask which of the two sons did his father's will. Though both imperfect, there is one who did the work he was called to do. After his emphatic no, he did something of great importance: he repented.

I'd love to be able to say I was a son that's not even mentioned—one who when given the orders to work said, "Yes, I'll go," and right away went, but I cannot say that. I have a feeling Jesus left that person out on purpose because he knew exactly where we would all fall.

The Bible doesn't share why the second son said no. Maybe his past mistakes caused his no; maybe it was his insecurities. What about you, Dear? What has caused your no? Or, what about your yes? What has caused you to commit only to quickly change your mind? How will we ever fulfill God's call on our lives if we aren't even working? Today, let's do what the first son did: Let's repent and get to work.

Called to Action

Ask:

Consider a time when your follow-through fell short of your declaration.

Am I even working in my Lord's vineyard?

Which son am I?

What has caused my no?

Continue Asking:

What do you want me to do before I die, Lord?

DAY TWENTY-THREE

THE UNPROFITABLE SERVANT

But he that had received one went and digged
in the earth, and hid his lord's money.
—Matthew 25:18 KJV

Those that have so much work to do, as every
Christian has, need to set about it quickly,
and lose no time.
—Matthew Henry

Jesus presented another parable to his disciples as he sat upon the Mount of Olives, recorded in Matthew 25. Instead of two sons, he used three servants. In this parable, he likened the kingdom of heaven to a man traveling to a far country.

Before departing, the traveler called his servants and delivered his goods to each of them according to their own abilities. Unto each servant, he gave talents (money). Five talents were given to the first, two to the second, and to the final man, one.

The story unfolds in verses fourteen through thirty as the first two servants put the money they were entrusted with to good use and both double their money. The last servant does not. After receiving his single talent, he is afraid so he digs a hole and hides his lord's money.

Which of the servants do you think did the right thing here?

At a glance, the first two could've been in the wrong. They took a risk with money that wasn't theirs to begin with. On the other hand, the last servant played it safe. In some ways, that may have seemed the best bet.

If I bury it, I can't lose it.

I don't know if that's what he thought, but I imagine I would have. None of the servants knew what time their lord would return. Two continued working while the other waited.

After a long time, the Bible says, the lord returned to settle accounts. His servants were about to hear two very different responses from him, and I have to wonder if they realized just how high the stakes were.

"Well done, good and faithful servant! You were faithful over a few things; I will put you in charge of many things. Share your master's joy."

The first two servants heard beautiful words of blessing, but much to his surprise, the last servant heard dreadful words.

"You wicked and slothful servant..." (Matt. 25:26 CSB).

The lord went on to tell him what he should have been doing while he was gone. He took away the talent the servant had buried and issued his defeating blow.

"And cast ye the unprofitable servant into outer darkness: there shall be weeping and gnashing of teeth" (Matt. 25:30 KJV).

The unprofitable servant.

It's hard to move past these three words because to me, that's what the entire story is really about. The Christian Standard Bible exchanges the word unprofitable for good-for-nothing.

The good-for-nothing servant. Ouch.

The original Greek word for unprofitable, *achreios,* means "useless," and I dare say that word needs no translation.

Matthew Henry breaks this parable down very simply. In his commentary of Matthew 24, he says, "The Master is Christ, who is the absolute Owner and Proprietor of all persons and things; into his hands all things are delivered. The servants are Christians, his own servants, so they are called; born in his house, bought with his money, devoted to his praise, and employed in his work."

In the parable, Jesus intentionally took time to share with his disciples that the master left his servants with something to do. Fellow Servants of Christ, so has our master.

The unprofitable servant hid the money because he was afraid. That excuse seems familiar to me. Does it to you? Matthew Henry says of the servant, "Had it been his own, he might have done as he pleased; but, whatever abilities and advantages we have, they are not our own, we are but stewards of them, and must give account to our Lord, whose goods they are."

The first two servants in this story understood that the money was not theirs. They took every opportunity to make good use of what they'd been given and to yield a greater return on their master's investment. There were risks involved but they were willing to take them.

Are we?

If you are reading this book, it is not too late. If you've hidden the talents God has given you, put the book down, grab your shovel and go dig them up. The Master has not yet returned, but he will, Beloved, he will.

Called to Action

Ask:

Have I buried what God has entrusted me with?

What am I afraid of?

Continue Asking:

Are you still asking the main question?

What does God want me to do before I die?

Do you already know one thing he wants you to do? Maybe you've always known. Maybe you're starting to get some ideas or maybe you have no idea at all. Either way, continue seeking, asking, and pondering.

DAY TWENTY-FOUR

YOU WANT US TO DO WHAT?

Now Abraham and Sarah were old and well stricken in age; and it ceased to be with Sarah after the manner of women.
—Genesis 18:11 KJV

Even true believers need to have God's promises doubled and repeated to them, that they may have strong consolation.
—Matthew Henry

"As for Sarah, your wife, I will bless her and give you a son by her."

Under most circumstances, hearing these words would have been met with great celebration, but when God spoke them to Abraham, there was a glaringly obvious problem. Sarah was ninety years old and Abraham was nearly a hundred. How could they possibly conceive and bear a child of promise at their age?

Abraham's reaction to God's news was rather dramatic: He fell on his face and laughed. Our minds aren't left to wonder what he was thinking.

"Can a child be born to a hundred-year-old man? Can Sarah, a ninety-year-old woman, give birth?" (Gen. 17:17 CSB).

The question that followed Abraham's laughter may not have been born of skepticism but of curiosity. He seemed to wonder if it was even physically possible at their ages.

Since God knows the thoughts and intents of man's heart without him speaking a word, he responded to Abraham's inaudible questions with a confirmation.

"Sarah, your wife, will bear you a son indeed..."

I love God's choice of words here. It's as if he's looking straight into Abraham's eyes and saying, "Oh yes! Sarah—YOUR wife."

God told Abraham what to name his son and reminded him of the everlasting covenant he'd establish with his seed. He spared few details in confirming the news to Abraham, even telling him when his wife would give birth the following year.

When a little doubt seemed to remain, the Lord appeared unto Abraham yet again in the form of three men in need of refreshments. Sarah was home when they arrived, so Abraham asked her to prepare bread while he went to get a calf.

"Where is Sarah, *your wife*?" One of the men asked as they ate. "I will certainly come back to you in about a year's time, and *your wife* Sarah will have a son!"

Well stricken in age and past the time of childbearing, Sarah stood at the tent door and heard the stranger's words. And, just like her husband, laughter preceded a question in her heart:

"After my husband and I are old, shall I have pleasure?"

To a barren woman, the thought of a child at any age must elicit pleasure. In spite of both Abraham and Sarah's laughter and questions, God asked one of his own:

"Is anything too hard for the Lord?" (Gen. 18:12-14 KJV)

Abraham and Sarah's story reminds me a bit of my own. After a difficult delivery, my firstborn son, Elijah, developed colic at two weeks of age. My introduction to motherhood was far from my expectations. For nearly nine months he screamed and cried. Nothing I did helped. I didn't have to think I'd lost my mind—I knew I had, because in the midst of the chaos, I became pregnant again.

On my son's first birthday, with his colic nearly gone, my husband and I announced we were having another baby. I was nervous but hopeful that the odds of another colicky baby were low. In the weeks that followed, I began having some concerning symptoms that led me to believe I was having a miscarriage. At the first ultrasound to see our baby, I feared there would be no heartbeat.

Cold gel hit my growing belly and my husband gasped.

"Is that what I think it is, doc?" my husband asked.

Turning the monitor towards me, my doctor responded.

"Yep, it's twins."

Tears took the place of Abraham and Sarah's laughter and they fell like rain down my cheeks as I lay there. I was still reeling from my first son's birth. My mental state had barely survived. I couldn't imagine how I would possibly manage three babies at once.

If Abraham or Sarah, the father and mother of nations, were to have asked God the question we're asking—what do you want us to do before we die?—I think we could all agree that they wouldn't have expected to hear what they did.

We're too old.

If I had asked the question earlier, I couldn't have imagined I would have twins or that I'd have three boys under eighteen months of age.

I'm completely incapable.

Have you noticed that God often calls us to do things we are completely unqualified to do? Just as Jesus was so good at doing, God asked a question in response to Abraham and Sarah's doubt that rings loudly.

Is anything too hard for the Lord?

When you begin asking yourself, "What does God want me to do before I die," be prepared. You just might hear things you never dreamed you'd hear.

Called to Action

Ask:

Has the fear of my own strength failing kept me from even moving at all?

Whose power am I relying on to accomplish what I've set out to accomplish?

Is anything too hard for the Lord?

Continue Asking:

What does God want me to do before I die?

DAY TWENTY-FIVE

GO BIG OR GO HOME?

Whatsoever thy hand findeth to do, do it with
thy might; for there is no work, nor device,
nor knowledge, nor wisdom, in the grave,
whither thou goest.
—Ecclesiastes 9:10 KJV

We are not here in vain, dear brethren.
—Charles Spurgeon

What does God want me to do before I die? Maybe we've never phrased the question quite like this but more than likely, we've asked it another way.

What am I supposed to be doing?

Lord, what is your calling for my life?

Ever the dreamer, I've had plenty of lofty visions. In my mind, only ideas on a grand scale seemed to count. Crowds of people, stages, foreign mission fields, you name it, I imagined it. God's call and the degree of his satisfaction with me—and frankly, my own as well—all hinged on my ability to find that elusive calling.

Eight years ago, when I thought I'd forever be as useless to God as a bag of rocks, I almost gave up on envisioning his call entirely. But as I cried out daily in desperation for wisdom, he was always (and remains) faithful to give it in unimaginable doses.

The call which I was so sure lay in cities or countries far away became evident in the sticky little mouths that kissed my own; in the perpetual flow of dirty dishes and even dirtier diapers; in the picking up of my husband's socks and in the making of dinner. The great call was right there all along.

My son's lifelong medical condition, short-gut syndrome, which followed more than thirteen surgeries (most of them bowel resections), left him with the inability to have bowel movements apart from diarrhea. Seventeen to twenty-one diapers, clothes, and carpet spots full of them each day to be exact. How could God's call be in diarrhea?

It was.

"Whatever your hand finds to do," the book of Ecclesiastes says, "do it with all your might." With my hands in sterile gloves, administering antibiotics through my son's central line, or at feeding therapy helping him learn to eat by mouth—those weren't the times for dreams of grandeur. That's where I was needed, and it was no less God's call.

In his sermon entitled "A Home Mission," Charles Spurgeon said, "I am persuaded that our home duties, the duties which come near to us in our own streets, in our own lanes and alleys, are the duties in which we ought most of us mainly to glorify Christ. Serve God in that which your hand findeth present. Serve Him in your immediate situation, where you now are. Just do that first which is nearest to you. Begin at home."

Sometimes what God wants us to do is on a scale so massive, if he showed us, we might pass out. Sometimes what he wants us to do is exactly what we're doing, even if we're elbow-deep in diapers. Go big or go home they say, but maybe it's the exact opposite. Maybe if we never start at home, we will never go big at all. Maybe our "big" will stay at home; judging by the ever-darkening world beyond our doors for which we must prepare our children, that in and of itself is a hefty call. Perhaps our callings will extend

beyond our homes. Whatever they are, they will still be God's calls, and that makes them extremely important.

Called to Action

Ask:

Do I struggle to see that God's call can also be in the ordinary stages of my life?

Am I content for them to be God's call even if they differ from my expectations?

Even when I know there's more, do I wait patiently?

Continue Asking:

What do you want me to do before I die, God?

DAY TWENTY-SIX

IF NOT YOU, WHO?

Ye have not chosen me, but I have chosen you, and ordained you, that ye should go and bring forth fruit, and that your fruit should remain...
—John 15:16 KJV

If not now, when? If not you, who?
—Hillel the Elder

"Joshua!"
"Brylie!"
"Elijah!"

Your hand wiggles back and forth and couldn't possibly be raised any higher as you wait to hear your name.

Pick me. Please, pick me next.

"Blakeley!"
"Isaiah!"

Fear turns into reality as the only other person left to be chosen for the game is selected.

"Brynlee!"

Left as the only option, you're finally called and reluctantly shuffle toward your team. You weren't chosen, you were tolerated.

Maybe it wasn't a sport or a game, but in one way or another, I'm sure you've felt this as a child and likely even as an adult.

What's worse than feeling rejected? I've been that child many times before and over the course of my life, unfortunately, I've feared rejection more than I've feared God.

As I read John 15:16, I was briefly transported to my school playground thirty years ago, where my fear of rejection and failure were higher than the big kid monkey bars. I could no more reach them than I could acceptance or confidence.

Five separate and important truths are contained in this one verse.

1. "Ye have not chosen me, but I have chosen you..." Unlike you, me, and children all over the world praying not to be picked last, we were chosen. Not just for a silly game of red rover or baseball, but for the greatest team ever assembled: the bride of Christ; the church. You—yes you—were hand-picked and selected as the very best to play a very important part.

2. "...and ordained you..." The Greek word for ordained, *tithemi*, means "to set, put, place." First God selected you, then he placed you.

3. "...that ye should go..." In spite of your fears, in spite of your failures, and in spite of your inabilities, you were chosen to go. As Matthew Henry's commentary on this verse says, "They [the disciples to whom Jesus was speaking] were ordained, not to sit still, but to go about, to be diligent in their work, and to lay out themselves unweariedly in doing good..."

4. "... and bring forth fruit..." Matthew Henry continues, "They were ordained, not to beat the air, but to be instrumental in God's hand for the bringing of nations into obedience to Christ." I grew up on a farm and to this day, my parents still farm and garden. I've noticed over the years that very little disappoints either of them more than to work hard tilling the ground, preparing the soil, and

planting and watering their seeds, only to watch their labor yield no fruit or flower at harvest time.

5. "...and that your fruit should remain..."

"Those whom Christ ordains should and shall be fruitful; should labour, and shall not labour in vain...that it might be perpetuated; that the fruit may remain; that the good effect of their labours may continue in the world from generation to generation, to the end of time," Matthew Henry stated.

From generation to generation. Oh, my.

To the end of time. Oh, me.

That's a lot of pressure I know, but aren't you and I here today because someone dear to us from another generation labored for fruit that remained?

No one else can do the job you've been called, chosen, and selected to do. It's your job; it's my job; and it is our great duty to do it to the very best of our ability. So, what is our job? What's our great duty? That's what we're in search of and that's why you're holding this book.

I am confident that God will show you if he hasn't already, but as you think of God's call and your duty, remember to ask yourself what lies at your hand to do. It may be as simple and as beautiful as preparing a meal for your family today. It may be helping a neighbor, reading your Bible, or praying for a loved one.

If you don't, who will?

Called to Action

Ask:

Do I know that I am chosen, selected and valuable?

Have I neglected duties or been lazy when I should have gone?

Is there evidence of fruit from my labor?

Am I laboring for fruit that will remain from generation to generation and to the end of time?

Continue Asking:

God, what do you want me to do before I die?

IT WASN'T SUPPOSED TO BE THIS WAY

But the God of all grace, who hath called us unto his eternal glory by Christ Jesus, after that ye have suffered a while, make you perfect, stablish, strengthen, settle you. To him be glory and dominion for ever and ever. Amen.
—1 Peter 5:10-11 KJV

Sometimes a grievous disappointment has changed the whole current of a person's life.
—Charles Spurgeon

I shivered against the cold air that cut right through my soaking wet clothes as I was wheeled from the car to the labor and delivery unit in the early morning hours of December 10, 2007.

I haven't set up the twin's nursery yet. They have no clothes or blankets. They don't even have names.

They're not ready. I'm not ready.

It wasn't supposed to be this way.

I wasn't supposed to go into premature labor. I wasn't supposed to have sick babies in the hospital. I wasn't supposed to watch one suffer and nearly die. I wasn't supposed to have my marriage and foundation rocked to their very core. I wasn't supposed to...

Or was I?

My list could go on and on and I'm sure yours could too. The disappointment of what *was* that I felt should not have been took years for me to process. The pain of what *was not* that I wanted to be took even longer. I allowed the disappointment and pain of that time to reign in my heart for years, and its effects were both devastating and paralyzing.

Thoughts of what God wanted me to do with my life were soon drowned out by the tune of "woe is me." I hate that melody, and yet I fell in its trap and sang it all day long.

By now, I should be doing _____.

I should have _____ *by now.*

Perhaps life has not gone in the direction you thought or hoped. Maybe deep disappointment has paralyzed you after being skipped over once again for a promotion. Maybe critical illness, betrayal, divorce, or the loss of someone you love deeply have stunted your growth.

What do you do when you don't know what to do? How do you live your purpose when you feel your purpose was ruined?

"Even in little things, we do not like to be disappointed. If our expectations are not realized, we feel as if a sharp thorn has pierced our flesh. But in great matters, disappointment is much more serious," said Charles Spurgeon in his sermon entitled "Maroth—or, the Disappointed."

Spurgeon continues, "Disappointments in this life, however, although they are at times very painful, are sometimes of such a character that could we know all the truth, we would not lament them. There are many who have looked forward to a change in their condition in life, or their position in society—and they have been disappointed. For a time they have been ready to wring their hands in anguish, yet if they knew what the consequences would have been if their expectations had been realized, they would fall down upon their knees and devoutly praise the Lord for the disappointment which had been so great a blessing in disguise to them! You, my brother, had expected to be rich by this time, but God knew that had you been rich, you would have been proud and worldly and would have ceased to enjoy fellowship with Him—so he kept you poor that you might still be rich in faith! You, my friend, had expected to be in robust health at this time, but had you been so, you might not have been walking so humbly before the Lord as you are now doing. Rest assured, O child of God, that whatever happens to you is as it should be! Believe that if you could have infinite wisdom, and the helm of your life's vessel could be entrusted to your hands, you would steer it precisely as God steers it! You would not always guide the ship through smooth water any more than He does. If you could be unerring in judgment and could be your own guide, you would choose for yourself the track which God has chosen for you. It is divine love and infallible wisdom that have ordered all things for you up to this very moment, so whatever your disappointments may have been, comfort yourself with the assurance that they have been among your greatest blessings."

I searched for a place in Spurgeon's sermon to cut off his quote but the richness of his text made it impossible. After reading it, I am reminded of Psalm 119:71KJV:

"It is good for me that I have been afflicted; that I might learn thy statutes."

How can affliction be good when it feels so bad? As parents it's so easy to see as we discipline our children. To them it feels awful; all the while, we know what character it's building. We can easily look past their discomfort and complaints because we know it's for their good. But oh, how hard is this concept to grasp when the tables are turned.

No matter how difficult they seem at the time, affliction, chastisement, and hard times are for our good.

- If Paul had not been seized and blinded, he would not have seen.
- If Jonah had not been swallowed by a large fish, the people of Nineveh would've perished.
- If Joseph hadn't been sold into slavery, his family would have starved to death.
- If Jesus had not bled and died, mankind would be lost.
- If we had not _____,
  _____ would not have happened.
- If we do not _____,
  _____ will never happen.

Called to Action

Ask:

Has the list of life's disappointments rocked you to your core?

Have you ever considered how they have or can fuel your very purpose, or have you allowed them to stop it all together?

Continue Asking:

God, what do you want me to do before I die?

DAY TWENTY-EIGHT

TAKE HEED, WATCH AND PRAY

*Take ye heed, watch and pray: for ye know
not when the time is.*
—Mark 13:33 KJV

*Personal consecration is the demand of the
age.*
—Charles Spurgeon

"Watch! Be alert! For you don't know when the time is coming." The CSB translation of this verse captures its essence well. There is an urgency noted, as well there should be.

In the garden of Gethsemane, Jesus asked his disciples for a special favor.

"My soul is exceeding sorrowful, even unto death: tarry ye here, and *watch* with me." (Matt. 26:38 KJV)

In the midst of an agony we cannot know, Jesus had a very important job for his men. He needed their help. Matthew Henry's commentary of this verse states that "what he said to them, he saith to all, watch. Not only watch for him, in expectation of his future coming, but watch with him, in application to our present work."

"What had become of us," he continues, "if Christ had been now as sleepy as his disciples were? It is well for us that our salvation is in the hand of one who *neither slumbers nor sleeps.* Christ engaged them to watch with him, as if he expected some succor

[aid] from them, and yet they slept; surely it was the unkindest thing that could be. When David wept at this mount of Olives, all his followers wept with him, but when the Son of David was here in tears, his followers were asleep. His enemies, who watched for him, were wakeful enough but his disciples, who should have watched with him, were asleep. Lord, what is man! What are the best of men, when God leaves them to themselves! Note, carelessness and carnal security, especially when Christ is in his agony, are great faults in any, but especially in those who profess to be nearest in relation to him. The church of Christ, which is his body, is often in an agony, fightings without and fears within; and shall we be asleep then?"

There is so much richness in what Henry just said. "What had become of us if Christ had been now as sleepy as his disciples were?" I shudder to think of it.

The church of Christ in agony and fightings from without and within. Shall we be asleep then? Oh, God, how clearly this is the state of today's church. Are we sleeping like the disciples did, or do we see what's happening?

What was once wrong is now right and what was right is now wrong. Schools once carried a sense of safety but now stand guarded by policemen watching for shooters. Malls and movie theatres have become battle zones.

Somewhere along the way, "You owe me" replaced "How can I help you."

Apathy and indifference moved in and overtook self-discipline and common courtesy. Within the church there is little difference as the lines between secular and sacred are blurred day by day. There are divisions, contentions, and blatant sin. What Matthew Henry said above bears repeating.

"Carelessness and carnal security, especially when Christ is in his agony, are great faults in any, but especially in those who profess to be nearest in relation to him."

We who profess to be Christians—who profess to be nearest to Christ—must first and at once examine our hearts. Oh, what damage we do when we are not at our posts, heeding, watching, and praying.

In his sermon entitled "Signs of the Times," Charles Spurgeon says, "I would charge each Christian to be doing everything that he can for his Lord, for his church, and for perishing sinners. Let each man do his own work in God's sight and in God's strength, each one taking care that the church does not suffer through any neglect on his part. Personal consecration is the demand of the age. These days of lethargy are times when living saints should feel intensely for sinners, when they should feel for them an anguish and an agony. In proportion as others grow callous, we must become sensitive. If ever we are to see better times, they must come through the intense earnestness of each separate believer crying out in pain for the souls of men, as one that travaileth in birth, till men be saved from everlasting burnings. May each Christian here feel this sacred anguish, and in addition may there be more intense and vigorous religious life in all. If we want to arouse others, we must be awake ourselves; if we would urge the church forward, we must quicken our pace; if we would stimulate a laggard church, we must ourselves throw our whole soul into the cause of God. Personal consecration daily deepened is the nearest way to promote the quickening of the entire church of God to a sense of her high calling. May the Holy Spirit invigorate us to the full force of grace, that we may be the means of awakening the whole church."

Do you sense the urgency? When you look around you, do you feel it? As you look within your heart, do you see the late hour? As important as finding the answer to our question is, what must surely precede it is the awakening we need in order to ask it. Dear One, we must ask it. We must feel more deeply this *sacred anguish* and pray earnestly that we *may be the means of awakening the whole church.*

We must.

Called to Action

Ask:

Are you awake or are you sleeping?

Do you dismiss the signs all around you?

As you near this book's end, I earnestly pray that if you were sleeping, by now you are no more. I trust the Holy Spirit has moved in your heart and begun to stir what has perhaps been stagnating.

If you were already wide awake and working, I pray that you have been stirred even more and encouraged to continue your work.

Continue Asking:

God, what do you want me to do before I die?

DAY TWENTY-NINE

SMALL BEGINNINGS

For who hath despised the day of small things?
—Zechariah 4:10 KJV

It is a very great folly to despise the day of small things, for it is usually God's way to begin His great works with small things.
—Charles Spurgeon

"How tiny is the seed that is sown in the garden, yet out of it there comes the lovely flower! How small is the acorn, but how great is the oak that grows up from it?" Charles Spurgeon understood the importance of small beginnings.

In his sermon entitled "Small Things Not to Be Despised," he continues, "God begins with men in the day of small things; He began so with us. How little and how feeble were we when first we came upon the scene of action. He that is now a giant was once so feeble that he could not move from place to place except as he was carried in his mother's arms. Let us, then, not despise the day of small things, as we see that God begins with little things in nature and among the sons and daughters of men. And I am sure that He does so in the great work of His Church. For what is the Christian Church compared with the great mass of the heathen world and of those who reject the Savior? Our Lord's method of spreading His truth among men was to begin with a handful of disciples in an upper room at Jerusalem, to fill them with His Spirit, and then to let them be scattered over the whole known world. This is usually God's plan of working, in His Church, and also in individual believers."

There is an order to things and in most cases, it starts small. "First the blade, then the ear, after that the full corn in the ear" (Mark 4:28 KJV). The blade must come before the ear and the ear before the corn inside the ear.

"You've got to crawl before you walk."

It's a phrase we've likely all heard and while its meaning is easy to understand, living it is not. Watching my children learn to walk was a hard process. Short, pudgy legs that had never held anything except love pats from Grandma were suddenly supposed to hold more than twenty pounds. The entire process was a wobbly mess, and no one escaped it without some bangs and bruises.

Some toddlers move from the crawling stage to standing slower than others. Sometimes their growth and progression have been stunted. When many other toddlers were walking, talking, and eating by mouth, my son lay in a hospital bed decorated with tubes. He couldn't even crawl—much less stand—but he couldn't help that. It wasn't his fault.

Are we not, Beloved, like these toddlers? Unsteady and uncertain, we put one foot in front of the other, terrifyingly unsure of whether our legs will buckle under the weight. Sometimes we do buckle. We weren't ready to walk yet, and we fell flat on our face. Other times, we're ready to stand but not quite ready to walk. We teeter and totter around, feeling our way through the awkwardness. Deep wounds have stunted our growth. From the outside it looks like we should be sprinting, and we try, but perhaps we need to go back and learn to crawl first. Perhaps our foundation wasn't quite what we thought it was and that has affected every stage since.

Matthew Henry said, "Christ's interest, both in the world and in the heart, is, and will be, a *growing* interest; and though the beginning be small, the latter end will greatly increase." Charles Spurgeon echoed his statement, saying, "It is within our souls as it is in the world without; the day begins with the dawn, but the shining light shines more and more unto the perfect day."

Your reach may start out small, but it will grow. No matter how wide it extends, hide not the light that is in you and see that it is ever growing. We don't light candles, the Bible says, to hide them under baskets. That would be absurd. We are to be a city on a hill, where the light of Christ that lives in us provides illumination for all around us to see.

Only God knows, Precious Saint, whether your reach be small or large; whether its distance be short or long. Can it be fully measured anyway? If only we could trace our own faith back to the sweet elderly grandmother or grandfather of ages gone by who knelt their feeble knees in the sand, pleading with God to save the household of their seed throughout all generations. Their contribution of prayer may have seemed small then, but here you and I are—me writing and you reading this book. Was their reach small to you?

To you, exhausted mother whose beginning seems small, whose hands are cracked and dry from dishes, whose eyes droop from sleep deprivation, and whose heart feels more chaos than love, your reach extends so much further than to the diaper tabs you fasten day in and day out.

To you, overworked and undervalued father whose calloused, hard hands remind you of the walls around your heart. Your worth is not in what you do, and though you may feel it goes unappreciated or unnoticed, it does not. Your reach touches your household every single day and it is deeply felt.

To you, child who longs to be seen and noticed, whose hands hold a phone or controller when your heart is crying for affection, you too are seen and not forgotten. As you reach out for a hug from your parents, its ripple goes straight to their hearts and says what words cannot.

Dear Mom,
Dad loves you but he's hurting and worn out too. He wants to tell you how he feels and how much he loves you, but he doesn't know how.

Dear Dad,
Mom appreciates you but she's exhausted. Her thoughts and emotions are not as clear as they used to be.

Dear Son and Daughter,
Mom and Dad see you and love you more than words can possibly express. The weight they carry on their shoulders is enormous and sometimes it gets heavier than they know how to hold.

Burst through the gates of your heart.
Fling wide open the doors that have long since been barred by pain and covered in caution tape. Though our reach may seem as small as our beginning, its impact may last a lifetime.

Called to Action

Ask:

Am I struggling through small beginnings? Am I content in them or do I wish them away?

Continue Asking:

God, what do you want me to do before I die?

DAY THIRTY

THE END OF A THING

*The end of a thing is better than its
beginning...*
—Ecclesiastes 7:8 NKJV

*Oh, infinitely better is the end of a spiritual
life than the beginning!*
—Charles Spurgeon

E tched in pen on my handmade flyer were the words
"Heaven or Hell." Inside was a plea for my neighbors to
think about eternity. I was far too young to fully grasp
death but even as a young girl, God put a heart within me to
consider its certainty. One day, convinced I needed to help others consider it too, I courageously set off to go door to door on
my bicycle with my neatly folded and carefully written appeal
in hand.

The heart seemed like such a simple thing to conquer as a
child. It was the place where love grew. Who couldn't use more
of that? As a little girl, boldly passing out my flyers, I couldn't
have known the depth of a heart. I never fathomed just how fragile, how painful, how beautiful, and how ugly the heart could
really be. The pain I would experience was shielded from my
view—and I am glad it was.

Writers will tell you that every good story has a beginning, a
middle, and an end. We are all somewhere along this spectrum,
both in life as a whole and in our specific circumstances. Charles

Spurgeon said, "You see that creeping worm, how contemptible is its appearance! You wish to sweep it away—that is the beginning of the thing. You see that insect with gorgeous wings playing in the sunbeams, sipping at the flower bells and full of happiness and life—that is the end thereof. That worm, that caterpillar, that maggot, if you will, is you! And you are to be content with that until you are wrapped up in the chrysalis of death."

Seeing the end of anything from the beginning can be hard. An artist with their blank canvas, a musician with their guitar, an architect with their blueprints, a writer with their blinking curser—I admire them all as they weave together what seems impossible to finish.

Sometimes the beginning is so difficult and so ugly we cannot fathom its end. When in the throes of motherhood, especially when my boys were young, I couldn't picture an end. Diapers, bottles, dirty clothes, and attitudes seemed never-ending. What I didn't realize is that in the process, I was being whittled, carved, and cut.

Charles Spurgeon continues in his sermon entitled, An Observation of the Preacher, "Again, you see that rough-looking diamond—it is put upon the wheel of the lapidary. With much care he begins to turn it and to cut it on all sides. It loses much— much that seemed to itself costly. Do you see it now? The king is to be crowned; the diadem is put upon the monarch's head with the trumpet's joyful sound. There is a glittering ray which flows from that diadem and it comes from that very diamond which was cut just now by the lapidary. You, Christian, may venture to compare yourself to such a diamond, for you are one of God's jewels. And this is the time of the cutting process. You must endure it. Be of good courage and murmur not. Let faith and patience do their perfect work. In the day when the crown shall be set upon the head of "the King eternal, immortal, invisible," one ray of glory shall stream from you, for you shall be His!"

Where are you in the narrative of life? Though we cannot know for sure, do you feel yourself to be in the beginning, the middle, or the end? Maybe you're just out of high school, uncertain of life's path. Perhaps you're a college student in debt, a young mother surrounded by children, or a young father working three jobs to take care of your family.

Fret not.

While we cannot know how soon an end will come to the state we are in, I am certain it will. Perhaps that end will not come as you think it will. The situation you are facing may not change, but the hurt and the anger it has caused your heart can. Elders, lay down your regrets of what might have been and pick up what is. What today holds is as ripe for good as it has ever been.

Just as beginnings have endings, so endings must have beginnings.

Charles Spurgeon, in his sermon entitled "An Observation of the Preacher," said, "It is very clear that we cannot have an ending if we have not a beginning. However bright our end might be, we can never know it experimentally unless we begin. The text, therefore, suggests the question to each one of us, Have I begun? Has God begun with me? The beginning may be dark and gloomy, but you can never have a bright ending without it. I know the beginning will involve the sacrifice of many pleasures and the giving up of friends—"pleasures" and "friends" so-called, but you cannot have an ending with the saints of God in Heaven unless you have a beginning with the poor and afflicted of His family on earth."

Though outwardly I no longer resemble the little girl that walked around her small town of Adairville, Kentucky going door to door knocking, inside, not much has changed. The heart of concern God gave me for others has never waned. I've exchanged my flyer for a book, but still I knock. Another knock comes too, and His is the one I beg you to hear.

"Behold, I stand at the door, and knock: if any man hear my voice, and open the door, I will come in to him, and will sup with him, and he with me" (Rev. 3:20 KJV).

Tap.

Tap.

Tap.

It is a gentle, patient knock upon your heart from your first love. First loves know the rawness and delicacy of our hearts. They know how scary it is to give ourselves with complete abandon. It takes extreme vulnerability. It takes courage. It will be harder for some than for others because your heart has been bruised and battered beyond recognition.

This book began when I heard a question.

"What do you want to do before you die?"

When I did, immediately in my heart, I heard another.

What does God want you to do before you die?

In my introduction, I shared my prayer that through this book you would discover at least one thing God wants you to do before you die. Have you, Friend? Are you pursuing it? We've been asking some very important questions for thirty days now. A lot has been expected of you and I thank you for your honesty and vulnerability. I'd like to leave you with a request for a favor—author to reader; believer to believer.

Please, I implore you, never stop asking what God wants you to do before you die, for I am fully persuaded he will show you as your story unfolds. May the question be in your heart like it is in mine—perpetual—and together, may we continue to

- perpetually ask
- perpetually go
- perpetually do

and perpetually be the sons and daughters of the living God, the hands and the feet that lead hurting and desperate hearts to the way to the Master, and the truth to future generations.

If God says the end of a thing is better than its beginning, rest assured it will be. Beloved, be of good courage and do what God wants you to do before you die, for much is at stake. If you have not seen it through the pages of this book, then I will write another, and another, and another. Our children, our children's children, and their children depend on it.

Printed in the United States
By Bookmasters